COMPLETE CONDITIONING FOR TENNIS

E. Paul Roetert, PhD
Managing Director
USTA Player Development

Todd S. Ellenbecker, DPT, CSCS
Clinic Director
Physiotherapy Associates, Scottsdale Sports Clinic

Human Kinetics

Library of Congress Cataloging-in-Publication Data

Roetert, E. Paul.
  Complete conditioning for tennis / E. Paul Roetert, Todd S. Ellenbecker.
    p. cm.
  Rev. ed. of: Complete conditioning for tennis. c1998.
  Includes index.
  ISBN-13: 978-0-7360-6938-0 (soft cover)
  ISBN-10: 0-7360-6938-0 (soft cover)
  1. Tennis--Training. 2. Exercise. I. Ellenbecker, Todd S., 1962- II.
United States Tennis Association. III. Title.
  GV1002.9.T7C66 2007
  796.342--dc22
                                        2007014000

ISBN-10: 0-7360-6938-0
ISBN-13: 978-0-7360-6938-0

Acquisitions Editor: Laurel Plotzke; **Developmental Editor:** Cynthia McEntire; **Assistant Editor:** Scott Hawkins; **Copyeditor:** Annette Pierce; **Proofreader:** Pam Johnson; **Indexer:** Dan Connolly; **Permission Manager:** Carly Breeding; **Graphic Designer:** Fred Starbird; **Graphic Artist:** Francine Hamerski; **Cover Designer:** Keith Blomberg; **Photographer (cover):** Nick Laham/Getty Images; **Photographer (interior):** Photos on pages 3, 73, 99, 188, 189, 190, 191, and 194 courtesy of the United States Tennis Association (USTA)/Lance Jeffrey. Photo on page 169 courtesy of the United States Tennis Association (USTA)/Michael Baz. Other interior photos Neil Bernstein, unless otherwise noted; **Photo Asset Manager:** Laura Fitch; **Visual Production Assistant:** Joyce Brumfield: **Photo Office Assistant:** Jason Allen; **Art Manager:** Kelly Hendren; **Illustrator:** Alan L. Wilborn; **Printer:** United Graphics

Human Kinetics books are available at special discounts for bulk purchase. Special editions or book excerpts can also be created to specification. For details, contact the Special Sales Manager at Human Kinetics.

Printed in the United States of America   10 9 8 7 6 5 4 3 2 1

Human Kinetics
Web site: www.HumanKinetics.com

United States: Human Kinetics
P.O. Box 5076
Champaign, IL 61825-5076
800-747-4457
e-mail: humank@hkusa.com

Canada: Human Kinetics
475 Devonshire Road Unit 100
Windsor, ON N8Y 2L5
800-465-7301 (in Canada only)
e-mail: orders@hkcanada.com

Europe: Human Kinetics
107 Bradford Road
Stanningley
Leeds LS28 6AT, United Kingdom
+44 (0) 113 255 5665
e-mail: hk@hkeurope.com

Australia: Human Kinetics
57A Price Avenue
Lower Mitcham, South Australia 5062
08 8372 0999
e-mail: info@hkaustralia.com

New Zealand: Human Kinetics
Division of Sports Distributors NZ Ltd.
P.O. Box 300 226 Albany
North Shore City
Auckland
0064 9 448 1207
e-mail: info@humankinetics.co.nz

COMPLETE CONDITIONING FOR TENNIS

Contents

DVD Contents vi

Preface ix

Acknowledgments xi

Key to Diagrams. xiii

Chapter 1   Meeting the Physical
Demands of Tennis 1

Chapter 2   Focused Training
for Solid Performance. 9

Chapter 3   High-Performance
Fitness Testing. 17

Chapter 4   Dynamic Warm-Up
and Flexibility 43

Chapter 5   Agility and Footwork 71

Chapter 6   Speed and Quickness 87

Chapter 7   Core Stability Training 97

Chapter 8 **Strength and Power Training** **113**

Chapter 9 **Aerobic and Anaerobic Training** **145**

Chapter 10 **Program Design** **153**

Chapter 11 **Solid Shoulder Stability** . . . **167**

Chapter 12 **Injury Prevention and Rehabilitation** **185**

Index **203**

About the Authors **207**

DVD Contents

Fitness Tests

One-Leg Stability Test

Medicine Ball Toss, Forehand and Backhand

Medicine Ball Toss, Overhead and Reverse Overhead

Hexagon Test

Spider Run Test

Dynamic Warm-Up and Static Stretching

Frankenstein Walk

Backward Step Over

Butt Kick

Inverted Hamstrings

Figure-4 Tuck

Side Lunge

Torso Rotation Into Lunge

Arm Hugs

Calf Stretch

Knees-to-Chest Stretch

Hamstring Stretch

Quadriceps Stretch

Hip Flexor Stretch

Piriformis Stretch

Posterior Shoulder Stretch

Chest Stretch

Sleeper Stretch

Speed, Agility, and Quickness Drills

Lateral Alley Drill

Forward and Backward Alley Drill

Lateral Cone Slalom

Forward and Backward Cone Slalom

Cross Cones

Figure 8

Four-Cone Square

Service-Box Crossover

Forward and Backward Horizontal Repeater

Vertical Repeater

Diagonal Repeater

Volley Drill

Forehand and Backhand Agility

Mini Tennis Z-Ball

High Knee March

Skip

Skip With Leg Extension

Ball Drop

Turn and Search

Core Stability Training

Abdominal Curl on Exercise
   Ball
Seated Ball Rotation
Side Plange

Knees to Chest
Knees to Chest With Rotation
Diagonal Leg Tuck

Strength and Power Training

Partial Squat
Lunge
Monster Walk
Calf Raise
Low-to-High Chop
Core Chest Press
Full Can
Bird Dog

Medicine Ball Pass
Wrist Flexion and Extension
Medicine Ball Tennis
Medicine Ball Squat
Plyometric Step Over
Medicine Ball Throw
Plyometric Chest Pass
Ball Dribble

Match Stamina

Turn, Turn, Turn
Forehand Only
Protect Your Turf

Transition Drill
Close and Drop

Shoulder Stability Test and Exercises

Shoulder Flexibility Test
90/90 Prone Plyometric
   Ball Drop
90/90 Plyometric Reverse Toss
Seated Row

External Rotation With
   Shoulder Retraction
Chest Punch
Standing External Rotation

Total Running Time . . . . 90 minutes

Preface

Welcome to *Complete Conditioning for Tennis*. Tennis has evolved as players, coaches, parents, and researchers have learned more about strength and conditioning and their impact on tennis performance. This book presents tennis-specific exercises in a practical form with a companion DVD so you can see the execution of the exercises and skills. *Complete Conditioning for Tennis* is a culmination of many years of work by top sports medicine and conditioning experts. Whenever possible, we have included research notes to support the principles behind the training programs.

The United States Tennis Association (USTA), the national governing body for tennis in the United States, promotes and develops the game and helps players move from one level to the next. The programs in this book are based on those developed by the USTA. Much of the information here is what top U.S. players have used to become stars at the U.S. Open Tennis Championships. The USTA staff tests, trains, and tracks the top American junior and professional players to provide them with the latest sport science information. This helps players with their performance and keeps them injury free.

Because the USTA has input over when and where certain junior and professional tournaments are held in the United States, it is able to schedule the most important tournaments at the optimal times of the year in the best locations. This greatly assists players in scheduling events. Although you may not have the luxury of scheduling tournaments, you can control your own schedule. As you will see in chapter 10, scheduling tournaments and fitting them in with your training schedule form the basis of effective periodization training. Periodization training allows you to schedule training to develop flexibility, strength, agility, speed, and other components of your conditioning program in the most effective manner.

Complete Conditioning for Tennis is divided into two major parts. The first nine chapters lay the foundation by providing the key components of a well-designed conditioning program. The second part provides tennis-specific programs that can be geared to your specific age, playing level, and conditioning background. We have incorporated as many exercises and examples as possible (don't forget to watch the DVD) to prepare you for both on- and off-court training.

We have been fortunate to be directly involved in the tennis business for more than 20 years and have conducted numerous studies related to conditioning tennis athletes. All of this allows us to provide you with the very latest, state-of-the-art training techniques. Our goal is to give you scientifically based information in an understandable and practical manner so that you can use it on the court immediately. We hope you enjoy this book and look forward to seeing you on the courts.

Acknowledgments

We would like to thank the USTA and its leadership for encouragement and allowing us the opportunity to take on this project.

Scott Riewald, PhD, USTA Administrator of Sport Science, contributed significant content to both the book and DVD. In addition, he kept this project on time and served as a liaison with the publisher. Both Scott and Mike Nishihara, USTA Strength and Conditioning Coach, provided many of the drills featured in both the book and DVD.

Both of us have been fortunate to spend time learning from and being around some of the top sport science, medical, and coaching experts in the world. Although we cannot thank each of these people individually, we are grateful for all of the opportunities that have been available to us.

Key to Diagrams

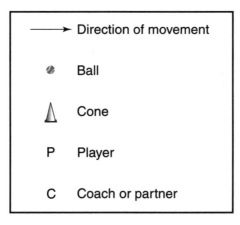

——→   Direction of movement

Ball

Cone

P   Player

C   Coach or partner

Chapter 1

Meeting the Physical Demands of Tennis

Watch the game of tennis today and you will be impressed by the fitness and physical prowess of the players. Consider some of the facts about a tennis match and you quickly see why they need this level of strength and conditioning.

- A tennis match can last anywhere from 30 minutes to several hours. In fact, several men's matches in the 2006 U.S. Open Tennis Championships lasted more than 4 hours. Even on the grass courts of Wimbledon, matches can last a long time. One set during a second-round match between Juan Carlos Ferrero and Radek Stepanek in 2006 lasted 83 minutes.

- Within the time period of a match, a tennis player can run 3 to 5 miles (5 to 8 kilometers).

- Most of those miles are spent moving short distances from side to side or forward and backward and sprinting in all directions.

- A typical tennis point lasts 3 to 7 seconds and requires a player to change direction several times.

- A tennis player performs 300 to 500 bursts of energy during a typical tennis match.

- The duration of a match clearly shows that tennis includes an aerobic component, yet the characteristics of frequently sprinting and changing direction point to a significant anaerobic component.

Many players enjoy the fitness benefits of playing tennis. However, to reach the next level of performance, players need to not only play tennis to get fit, but more important, need to get fit to play tennis. It is estimated that up to 75 percent of all strokes hit at the professional level are serves and forehands, meaning certain muscle groups do the bulk of the work in a match. Add to that the various surfaces played on, the use of open stances and powerful strokes, and the repetitive nature of the game, and it becomes clear that a proper conditioning program to help players enhance performance while staying injury free is imperative. *Complete Conditioning for Tennis* outlines conditioning programs that will allow all players to achieve that goal.

This book lays out the components of a conditioning program, such as flexibility, strength, power, agility, and speed, and recommends ways to improve each trait in practical terms. These key components are listed and described here and expanded on throughout the book. The bottom line is that tennis players need a little bit of everything to be successful, and our goal is to help you develop these components of your game by helping you design a tennis-specific strength and conditioning program.

FLEXIBILITY

Tennis requires a player to hit the ball from some pretty amazing positions. Watch any match with Kim Clijsters and you will likely see her run wide for a ball and actually go into the splits to get that extra bit of extension she needs to get to the ball. This requires a great deal of flexibility.

Although you may never do the splits on court, flexibility is just as much a part of your game. Think about the positions you do get in on the court: extending the body to reach a wide ball, reaching to retrieve a lob, lunging forward to cover a drop shot. All these positions require flexibility. To perform at your best, your muscles must be strong through a full range of motion. Any restrictions in flexibility will limit your movement efficiency and may also restrict how much force your muscles can generate. Having good flexibility (see chapter 4 for more details on flexibility) can also help prevent injury. Tennis is played on a variety of surfaces and your opponent is trying to move you all around the court, forcing you to make off-balance shots from all posi-

Kim Clijsters reaching for a wide ball.

tions. Having good flexibility will help you get to balls more quickly and efficiently while setting up to hit with both balance and control.

STRENGTH AND POWER

Watch how hard today's players hit the ball and you quickly realize that both strength and power are important for players to reach the top of their game. Andy Roddick, for example, has hit a serve at 157 miles per hour (mph) (253 kilometers per hour [kph]) and regularly tops 130 mph (209 kph), even in the last games of a 5-set match. Serena Williams uses her strength and power to rip backhand winners from essentially anywhere on the court. You are no different: Your game will improve as you become stronger and more powerful. The speed of the ball seems to increase every year, and players need to be able to handle the power produced by their opponents and generate power themselves.

Strength has to do with how much force your muscles can generate and power relates to explosiveness, or how quickly you can generate those forces. The United States Tennis Association (USTA) looks at strength from two perspectives. First and most important, you must have sufficient muscular strength, particularly in the legs, core, upper back, and shoulders, to handle the forces of the game and be able to play injury free. Because tennis is a game of repetition, performing the same movements over and over again, it is easy to develop strength imbalances throughout the body that can contribute to injury. Having a base level of strength in all muscles, not just those used to make the ball go, is important for maintaining proper joint mechanics and muscular balance. Once this base level of force is established, players work to develop greater strength and power to enhance performance on the court.

With a base level of strength established, you can then work on developing power (the second aspect). Both upper-body and lower-body power are important in tennis. For example, having an explosive first step allows you to cover the court more efficiently, and being able to explode with the legs allows you to maximize the power in your serve. Similarly, having power in the core and shoulder allows you to generate power behind virtually any groundstroke.

Andy Roddick's powerful serve.

Strength and power do not come naturally in tennis. In fact, to truly maximize these aspects of your game, you have to do more than just play tennis. Consequently, all tennis players should incorporate exercises that build strength and power into their training programs, first to prevent injuries and second to enhance performance.

MUSCULAR ENDURANCE

One of the best ways to prevent injuries is to develop muscular endurance. Players need to be able to use the same muscles over and over, ideally being able to hit the ball with the same amount of force at the end of the match as at the start of the match. When you consider that a 5-set match can last more than 4 hours, it is easy to see how important muscular endurance is in tennis.

Throughout this book, many of the tennis-specific exercises use a high number of repetitions. This addresses the important component of muscular endurance and is based on the needs of the tennis player.

AGILITY AND SPEED

A typical 5-second point in tennis requires more than four changes in direction, making agility, or the ability to change direction quickly and effectively, a critical component of the game. Being able to start and stop quickly provides more time to get into position and set up for the next ball. Agility also relates to movement efficiency and therefore allows a player to save energy throughout a match.

Speed, the ability to get from point A to point B rapidly, is also important in tennis. Being fast allows a player to get to more balls and set up with more time to prepare. To some degree, speed is genetically determined; players with more fast-twitch muscle fibers will generally be able to generate more force and will be faster. However, all players can improve speed by performing exercises and drills designed to build speed. (See chapter 6 for more on developing speed.) These drills train the muscles and the nervous system to react quickly. Remember, the faster you can get to the ball, the more time you will have to set up for the next shot.

Serena Williams sprinting toward the net.

©Nick Laham/Getty Images

BODY COMPOSITION

Body composition refers to the makeup of the body—how much fat, muscle, bone, and water the body contains. The amount of bone and water remains relatively constant, so to alter body composition, you need to think about the amount of muscle mass and fat you carry around.

Female tennis players should shoot for a body-fat percentage of 15 to 25. Men should strive for 8 to 18 percent. Strength training will add muscle mass, but you also need to eat healthy foods and engage in regular aerobic exercise (like tennis) to lose body fat.

Although tracking body weight will give you some indication of how well you are doing as you try to change body composition, weight alone does not tell the whole story because muscle weighs more than fat. It is possible to lose fat and still gain weight if you are also adding muscle to your frame. Usually a look in the mirror will tell you if you are making the body composition changes you desire.

Tennis players should not get caught up in the many fad diets that are available, including the numerous low-carbohydrate diets. Carbohydrate provides fuel and energy for the body and is essential for a tennis player. Taking it out of your diet will affect your energy level and your ability to sustain a high level of intensity for prolonged periods. A proper diet, aerobic exercise (like tennis), and strength training will make your body composition goals attainable.

STABILITY AND DYNAMIC BALANCE

Stand on one foot. If you do not fall over you may think you have a pretty good sense of balance. Now, while balancing on one foot, slowly lower your body into a partial-squat position. If you are like most people you will find that maintaining your balance during movement, a movement characteristic called *dynamic balance,* is more difficult than staying balanced in a stationary position. Think how much more difficult it is to balance when moving at high speeds during a tennis match.

Dynamic balance is a difficult skill to master, and yet it is this ability that allows you to maintain control of your body when hitting difficult shots. As the speed of the game continues to increase,

Rafael Nadal hitting an off-balance shot.

©Greg Wood/Getty Images

players find they have to hit more and more off-balance shots. Having good dynamic balance will allow you to play with control and be able to hit shots with power and accuracy, even when on the run.

AEROBIC AND ANAEROBIC FITNESS

Is tennis an aerobic, or endurance, sport, or is it an anaerobic sport? The body's aerobic energy system provides fuel to muscles for endurance events, activities lasting longer than several minutes. The anaerobic energy system provides energy to fuel short, high-intensity bursts of activity. Tennis play fits into both definitions.

A typical point in tennis, even when played on clay, the slowest court surface, lasts fewer than 10 seconds; most last fewer than 5 seconds. During a match, a player may have to generate 300 to 500 bursts of energy, sprinting to get to the ball and tapping into the anaerobic energy system to fuel the muscles during each high-intensity effort. This makes it pretty clear that tennis is a sport that relies primarily on the anaerobic energy system, right? Well, that's not the whole picture.

Think about the entire match. A match can easily last an hour or more, which makes it an endurance activity, relying predominantly on the aerobic energy system. Additionally, while you may go all out for the 5 to 10 seconds that a point is being played, there are 25 seconds between points and 90 seconds during a changeover. During this time, the aerobic energy system takes over to replenish energy stores. Someone with poor aerobic fitness will find it difficult to recover between points and is likely to be tired at the end of the match. So, armed with this evidence, we can say tennis is primarily an aerobic activity, right?

In reality, both the aerobic and anaerobic energy systems are important in tennis and should be trained appropriately. A properly designed training plan will incorporate aerobic training and anaerobic training, the amount of each being determined by your current level of fitness and your style of play.

TESTING, TRAINING, AND TRACKING

How do you know which aspects of your game you need to work on and how do you know if you are making the improvements that will take your game to the next level? To find the answer, follow a three-part plan: *testing, training, and tracking.*

First, undergo periodic testing to identify your strengths and weaknesses. Test as many of the physical components of tennis as possible—flexibility, speed, power, agility, endurance, and so on. Refer to chapter 3 for tests to evaluate your fitness.

Once you identify areas that need work, structure your training to work on those areas. If you need to work on endurance, focus on getting more aerobic training. If power is lacking in your game, include plyometric exercises to build explosiveness. Each player will have a slightly different program to target his or her specific needs.

Finally, track your progress. Do you notice that you have more energy at the end of a match after two months of increased aerobic training? Do you find you have a quicker first step and are getting to more balls? This subjective assessment is important, but so is retesting yourself using the same battery of fitness tests. Keep a record of how well you are doing and use this information to adjust the focus of your training.

Player performing the Spider Run to gauge his quickness and agility.

PROGRAM PLANNING—PUTTING IT ALL TOGETHER

Whether you're a professional player chasing a top 10 world ranking, a developing junior player, or a recreational player who plays doubles several times per week, you can benefit from tennis training and planning how everything fits together. Those who have been around the sport scene for a while may have heard the term *periodization*. This term describes how to set up a schedule that takes your goals, competition schedule, training, and, most important, rest into account. The principles behind periodized training are solid and have been shown to elevate performance in a variety of sports, including tennis.

One of the best approaches to designing a training plan is to work back from your major competitions—when do you want to be at your best? With that established, you need to identify a period of time, or several periods, to devote to putting in the work and building a base level of strength. As you get closer to your major competition, make your training more tennis specific, boosting the intensity while dropping the volume of work. Also, realize that you cannot perform at 100 percent all the time. Schedule regular rest into your training plan.

When planning your training, consider your game style, how you play the game of tennis. Are you a serve-and-volleyer who looks to end points quickly at the net? If so, you may want to focus on power development and anaerobic training. Are you a counterpuncher whose approach is to outlast your opponent and force him or her to make mistakes? If so, aerobic conditioning and muscular endurance may be more important to you than developing power.

We will go into each of these areas in greater detail when we discuss periodized training in chapter 10, but it is important to know there is a method to the madness of strength training and conditioning.

SUMMARY

Use the information in this book to design your own training plan, one tailored to your needs and playing style. Each component of tennis fitness will be discussed in greater detail in the chapters to come. This overview, however, highlights the multifaceted demands tennis imposes on the human body and the important areas of emphasis for training and conditioning. The remaining chapters will provide greater detail for players of all levels to prevent injury and enhance performance.

Chapter 2

Focused Training for Solid Performance

The way tennis is played has changed significantly over the past 30 years. Specifically, we have seen quite a few changes in tennis technique as players have traded closed stances and eastern grips for open stances and western grips. Racket technology has also, at least partially, been responsible for players at the top level hitting the ball harder and from more open stances. Serves are being hit at 130 miles (209 kilometers) per hour (sometimes even harder) and both forehands and backhands are used as major weapons from almost anywhere on the court.

To be able to handle these modern strokes, players need a solid base of muscular strength, flexibility, endurance, and power. To enhance performance and promote injury-free play, proper technique is a must for both effective and efficient play. This relates to on-court movement as well as the tennis strokes themselves. The field of biomechanics, the study of forces and their impact on movement, helps players understand the science of tennis technique.

A knowledge of biomechanics directly affects a player's understanding of the technique and training needed for tennis. The human body has 600 muscles and 206 bones held together by tendons and ligaments. All of these structures have to work in a coordinated manner to produce the correct joint actions for each tennis stroke. A tennis player tries to coordinate the muscles, and the forces they generate, in the lower body, torso, and upper body while swinging a racket. The goal of any tennis player is to do this in the most effective and efficient manner possible. Add to this the fact that athletes play on a variety of court surfaces using one of several game styles, and you can see that mastering proper technique can be quite an achievement.

GAME STYLES

It is important to understand your game style so that you can design a proper training program. A player who runs around the court and retrieves balls the entire match will need a lot of muscular endurance, whereas someone who frequently serves and volleys will have to focus on developing muscular power. At the same time, both game styles require excellent flexibility.

Although there are many ways to classify game styles, we typically break them into four major categories: counterpunchers, aggressive baseliners, all-court players, and serve-and-volleyers. As described in the USTA book *Tennis Tactics* (Human Kinetics, 1996), *counterpunchers* usually have excellent movement skills, demonstrate quickness, and hit steady groundstrokes, accurate passing shots, and well-controlled lobs. Therefore, superb conditioning, particularly aerobic fitness and muscular endurance, is a must for a player adopting a counterpunching game style. An *aggressive baseliner* needs quickness, muscular strength, endurance, and power to engage in long baseline rallies while being able to hit winners with power. Good footwork and steady balance are also key characteristics of this style of play. *All-court players* are typically athletic, quick, and have excellent movement skills enhanced by endurance and a high level of muscular fitness to be able to cover the entire court. *Serve-and-volleyers* are often most comfortable at the net, where they need to possess a good reach, agility, a powerful overhead, and a soft touch. Although all players, regardless of game style, will require flexibility, strength, power, endurance, and balance, knowing your game style will help you individualize a training program based on your particular style.

Maria Sharapova, an aggressive baseliner, stretches to return a shot. Develop a training program around your style of play.

MOVEMENT IN TENNIS

Tennis requires players to move quickly in all directions, change directions often, and stop and start abruptly, all while maintaining the balance and control needed to hit the ball effectively. Properly designed training exercises, including strength and flexibility exercises, are critical for injury prevention. The sprinting, stopping, starting, and bending required by tennis play repeatedly subjects the bones, ligaments, and muscles to high loads, and they must be able to absorb these forces. The key to hitting a tennis stroke successfully over and over is to use proper mechanics and remain balanced while doing so. Proper mechanics can be learned by taking lessons from a teaching professional and grooving a specific swing pattern. Equally important is the ability to get to the ball.

The legs generate much of the power behind a tennis shot. Therefore, improving both strength and flexibility in the legs is important. In fact, this forms the basis of the Spanish training system. Spain's development program for up-and-coming juniors is founded on movement-based drill sessions in the morning followed by playing sets in the afternoon, mostly on clay courts. In addition, players perform off-court training sessions to supplement these on-court workouts. Many top young American players have started focusing on this type of program as well. Speed, agility, and quickness allow a player to arrive at each shot in a balanced position. This balanced position, in turn, allows the player to use proper technique on every shot and to prepare quickly for the next shot.

> ## CONDITIONING TIP
>
> Research shows that of the various physical components needed to be a good tennis player, agility and speed are the best predictors of success in young tennis players.

MUSCLE ACTIONS

It is important to understand the various muscle actions used on the court so that a strength and flexibility training program can properly prepare the body for the tennis-specific stresses of a match. Most activities on the court either shorten or lengthen the involved muscle groups.

In *concentric* muscle actions, the muscle fibers contract and shorten. An example of this type of muscle action is the shortening of the muscles in the front of the shoulder and chest when hitting a forehand. An *eccentric* muscle action occurs when the muscle fibers lengthen under tension. In that same forehand, the muscles of the back of the shoulder and upper back lengthen under tension to protect the shoulder and to make sure the follow-through stays controlled. Eccentric muscle actions help decelerate body segments and assist the body in shock absorption and stabilization. Eccentric contractions are also important for storing elastic energy in

©Sport the Library

Rafael Nadal chases a ball. Leg strength and flexibility are key to setting up and returning the ball from a balanced position.

muscles. As an active muscle is stretched, it stores energy, much like a rubber band.

In many cases, these eccentric contractions are followed by concentric contractions, releasing the energy that was stored and allowing a player to produce an extra bit of muscular force. This is particularly true for the lower body. Picture, for instance, a player performing a split step. The purpose of the split step is to prepare the body for an explosive movement in any direction while maintaining proper balance. As the player performs the split step, the muscles are lengthened under tension (eccentric contraction). This action is immediately followed by the player moving toward the oncoming ball (concentric contraction). Similarly, in the serve, the quadriceps muscles in the front of the upper leg lengthen during knee flexion and shorten during knee extension while driving the body and racket up for the ball.

> ### CONDITIONING TIP
>
> In tennis players, one side of the upper body tends to be stronger than the other. However, muscular strength in both legs is relatively equal.

To see the storage of elastic energy in action you can do a simple experiment involving a vertical jump. Research has shown that athletes jump higher after performing a countermovement (rapidly flexing the knees and hips, allowing the body to drop slightly) before jumping compared to jumping from a static position (getting into the starting position and holding that position before jumping). The muscles are not stronger in either scenario. However, the elastic energy stored by the leg muscles during the countermovement gives the impression that they are stronger. It is important to take advantage of this free strength whenever possible.

Storing elastic energy in the legs through the coordinated effort of eccentric and concentric contractions assists in the transfer of forces from one body part to the next. In fact, the concept of transferring forces from the ground up all the way to the racket is one of the most important to understand when analyzing tennis technique and the key to effective and efficient tennis strokes. It is called the kinetic-link principle, kinetic chain, or linked system of transferring forces.

In many instances, muscles also contract *isometrically,* meaning they do not change length during the contraction. Imagine standing and pressing your hands together in front of your chest as hard as you can. Unless you are really a lot stronger on one side of your body than the other, no motion will occur. Your muscles are not changing length, but they definitely are working. Many of the stabilizing muscles in your body, such as the core or the muscles that stabilize the shoulder blades, work this way. They contract isometrically to provide stability and keep one body part from moving relative to another. All three types of contractions are used in tennis, and you should train all three in a strength and conditioning program for tennis.

> **CONDITIONING TIP**
>
> Approximately 50 percent of stored energy is lost if there is a pause of as little as 1 second between the backswing (storing of elastic energy) and forward-swing (releasing that elastic energy) phases of a stroke.

COORDINATED MOVEMENT

The kinetic-link or kinetic-chain principle is probably the most important principle to understand as it relates to tennis technique. The goal is to have smooth, efficient strokes on the court to help you play without the risk of injury.

The goal, particularly in the serve and groundstrokes, is to transfer forces from body segment to body segment in an orderly fashion so that each segment benefits from what was done by the previous segments (see figure 2.1). In other words, forces are generated from the ground up through leg flexion and extension. These forces are transferred to the next segment in the system—the trunk. As the trunk rotates forward, the upper extremity (hitting arm) starts its forward motion and continues the process by transferring the forces to the racket and ball. This sequence of events must be completed in this order and with precise timing and coordination to maximize the contributions made by each link in the kinetic chain.

Leaving out or poorly timing any of the segments will reduce the force production, while also placing greater loads on the smaller muscle groups that make up the links closer to the end of the kinetic chain. This excessive

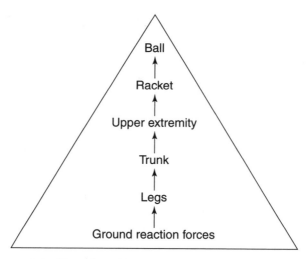

Figure 2.1   Transfer of forces through the kinetic chain.

loading could lead to injury. Think about it. The biggest and strongest muscles in the body are located in the legs and trunk. It makes sense to use them rather than just the smaller muscles of the shoulder and arm to generate the power behind your strokes. Efficiency of movement will also allow a player to conserve energy, which becomes a tremendous benefit in long matches.

MUSCLES USED IN STROKE TECHNIQUE

So which muscles are most important for tennis players to train? As you will see in chapter 8, quite a few exercises serve the needs of tennis players, and different exercises serve different purposes. For example, you want to make sure that the muscle groups providing the power for each shot are well prepared. In addition, you want to make sure that you have developed the endurance of the muscles. Finally, you want to make sure to train the muscle groups that oppose the muscles that generate force. Certain muscles work eccentrically, meaning that they lengthen under stress (e.g., muscles of the upper back and back of the shoulder when hitting a serve or forehand). A properly designed

Roger Federer not only demonstrates strong tennis skills but also a commitment to training and fitness.

training program will contain exercises to help prepare these muscles for action. Tables 2.1, 2.2, and 2.3 list the various muscles involved in the tennis strokes.

Table 2.1 Muscular Activity During the Forehand Groundstroke

Action	*Muscles used*
Loading phase	
Lower-body push off	Gastrocnemius, soleus, quadriceps, gluteals (concentric)
Trunk rotation	Obliques, abdominals, back extensors (concentric and eccentric)
Forward swing	Anterior deltoid, subscapularis, biceps, serratus anterior, pectoralis major, wrist flexors, forearm pronators (concentric)
Follow-through phase	
Lower body	Gastrocnemius, soleus, quadriceps, gluteals (eccentric)
Trunk rotation	Obliques, back extensors, abdominals (concentric and eccentric)
Arm deceleration	Infraspinatus, teres minor, triceps, serratus anterior, rhomboids, trapezius, wrist extensors, forearm supinators (eccentric)

Reprinted, by permission, from "Training Muscles for Strength and Speed" by Todd Ellenbecker and Craig Tiley in *World-Class Tennis Technique*, edited by Paul Roetert and Jack Groppel, Champaign, IL: Human Kinetics, page 64.

Table 2.2 Muscular Activity During the One-Handed Backhand Groundstroke

Action	*Muscles used*
Acceleration phase	
Lower-body push off	Gastrocnemius, soleus, quadriceps, gluteals (concentric)
Trunk rotation	Obliques, abdominals, back extensors (concentric and eccentric)
Forward arm swing	Infraspinatus, teres minor, posterior deltoid, rhomboid, serratus anterior, trapezius, triceps, wrist extensors (concentric)
Follow-through phase	
Trunk rotation	Obliques, back extensors, abdominals (concentric and eccentric)
Arm deceleration	Subscapularis, pectoralis major, biceps, wrist flexors (eccentric)

Reprinted, by permission, from "Training Muscles for Strength and Speed" by Todd Ellenbecker and Craig Tiley in *World-Class Tennis Technique*, edited by Paul Roetert and Jack Groppel, Champaign, IL: Human Kinetics, page 64.

Table 2.3 Muscular Activity During the Serve and Overhead

Action	Muscles used
Loading phase	
Lower-body push off	Gastrocnemius, soleus, quadriceps, gluteals (eccentric)
Trunk rotation	Obliques, abdominals, back extensors (concentric and eccentric)
Cocking phase	
Trunk extension and rotation	Back extensors (concentric); obliques (concentric and eccentric); abdominals (eccentric)
Arm motion	Infraspinatus, teres minor, supraspinatus, biceps, serratus anterior, wrist extensors (concentric); subscapularis, pectoralis major (eccentric)
Acceleration phase	
Lower body	Gastrocnemius, soleus, gluteals, quadriceps (concentric); hamstrings (eccentric)
Trunk rotation	Abdominals, obliques (concentric); back extensors (eccentric)
Arm motion	Subscapularis, pectoralis major, serratus anterior, triceps, wrist flexors, forearm pronators (concentric); biceps (eccentric)
Follow-through phase	
Lower body	Gastrocnemius, soleus, quadriceps, gluteals (eccentric)
Trunk rotation	Back extensors (eccentric); obliques, abdominals (concentric/eccentric)
Arm deceleration	Infraspinatus, teres minor, serratus, trapezius, rhomboids, wrist extensors, forearm supinators (eccentric)

Reprinted, by permission, from "Training Muscles for Strength and Speed" by Todd Ellenbecker and Craig Tiley in *World-Class Tennis Technique*, edited by Paul Roetert and Jack Groppel, Champaign, IL: Human Kinetics, page 65.

SUMMARY

It is clear that proper technique can help players hit the ball more efficiently and effectively. Training the appropriate muscle groups correctly is the basis of a well-designed training program. Getting in position for the ball (you can't hit it if you can't get to it) allows for proper balance in setting up for each shot, and sequencing the correct body parts in each of the strokes allows for the efficient transfer of forces. Although there may not be one correct form for hitting the ball, several key positions and movements are common to all efficient stroke patterns. These fundamentals of movement form the basis of proper technique.

The next important step of a well-designed training program is to test players regularly and to keep track of each player's test results. That's covered next in chapter 3.

High-Performance Fitness Testing

What makes Roger Federer and Rafael Nadal such great tennis players? Their skill level is obviously outstanding. They hit great serves, groundstrokes, and volleys. They have amazing power but also have the ability to maintain their power throughout long matches, demonstrating remarkable endurance as well. In addition to hitting the ball well, they also work very hard on their physical fitness.

No matter what your ability, you can't play your best tennis if you're not physically fit. Being physically fit means that your heart, blood vessels, lungs, and muscles can function at maximum efficiency. When you are fit, your body adjusts more easily to increased physical demands. Another important component of proper fitness is injury prevention. It is impossible to develop your game and hone your on-court skills if you are injured.

In this chapter we outline tests you can use to evaluate and monitor your fitness and assess key parts of your musculoskeletal system in order to prevent injury and enhance your performance.

USTA FITNESS AND PERFORMANCE TESTING PROTOCOL

The United States Tennis Association (USTA) has identified the essential components of fitness and injury prevention—flexibility, strength and power, muscular endurance, agility and speed, body composition, stability and dynamic balance, and aerobic and anaerobic fitness—and designed a testing protocol based on these components. Keeping track of your testing results can help you pinpoint strengths and weaknesses, design or refine a training program, and monitor your progress. Based on the results of testing many junior tennis players, the USTA has established four categories divided by age group and gender for each test: excellent, good, average, and needs improvement. Each category provides a range you can use when setting goals and interpreting your test results. From your test results you can determine which fitness area needs improvement for the purposes of injury prevention and performance enhancement.

FLEXIBILITY

Flexibility is the motion available (how far you can move around) at a joint, such as the shoulder, elbow, wrist, hip, knee, and ankle. See chapter 4 for a complete discussion of flexibility and how to improve it.

Few people are as flexible around all of their joints as they need to be. Tennis places tremendous demands on various body parts by requiring extremes of motion, for example, fully extending your arm over your head to reach for a lob. Throughout a match you are called on to generate great force from a variety of body positions: changing direction, reaching for a shot, stopping quickly, and serving are just a few examples. Strength throughout a flexible, unrestricted range of motion will help prevent injury and enhance performance.

FLEXIBILITY TESTING

Sit-and-Reach

Are you able to touch your toes while keeping your knees straight? If not, you are like many tennis players who have poor lower-back flexibility. Research has shown that on the men's professional tennis tour, 38 percent of players have missed at least one tournament because of lower-back problems. Hitting tennis balls not only involves a lot of body extension, but also a lot of twisting. The key to having good flexibility is to stretch your muscles regularly (see chapter 4). This will help you prevent injuries and reach the wide shots that you could not get to before. How do you know if you are flexible enough? Take a sit-and-reach test and see if you can reach past your toes. This test measures the flexibility of the lower back and hamstrings.

Procedure

1. Sit with your knees extended and legs flat on the floor. Have a partner hold your knees so they do not come off the floor.
2. Lean forward with your arms extended and have your partner measure the distance from your fingertips to your toes. Your hands should be placed next to each other with your index fingers touching.
3. Record your score. If you reach your toes, record a zero. If you do not reach your toes, record the distance between your fingertips and toes

in negative inches. If you reach past your toes, record the number of inches between your fingertips and toes in positive inches.

4. Look up your score on table 3.1.

Table 3.1 Sit-and-Reach (in inches*)

	Female		Male	
	Adult	Junior	Adult	Junior
Excellent	>6	>8	>3	>4
Good	4–6	7–8	1–3	2–4
Average	2–4	5–7	0–1	1–2
Needs improvement	<2	<5	<0	<1

*1 inch = 2.5 centimeters

Hip Flexor Flexibility

The hip flexors are important muscles that originate on the spine and cross the front of your hip joint. Because of the postures maintained and positions used during tennis play (such as the slight lean forward in an athletic posture, or ready position), hip flexor tightness is common among high-level players. Additionally, tightness of the hip flexors and quadriceps can cause lower-back dysfunction and decrease a player's lower-body power and movement capability.

Procedure

1. Lie on your back on a treatment table so that both of your legs hang over the edge of the table, with the edge of the table hitting the middle of your thighs.
2. Bring both knees up toward your chest.
3. Holding one leg against your chest, let the other leg drop over the edge of the table (figure 3.1).
4. Achieving neutral hip extension requires that the thigh touch the table. Inability to achieve neutral hip extension indicates lack of flexibility in the hip flexors. To quantify the inflexibility, use a goniometer to measure the angle between the thigh and the torso. To assess the length, and therefore flexibility, of the rectus femoris on the

Figure 3.1

front of the thigh, attempt to bend the knee of the lowered leg to a 90-degree angle without causing the hip to flex and raise the thigh off the table. Keep the leg not being tested against your chest during these maneuvers.

Hamstring Flexibility

Note: This test should be administered by a trained professional such as a physical therapist or athletic trainer.

Hamstring flexibility measures the amount of stretch in the muscle in the back of the thigh. Tennis players use this muscle to stop, start, run, and jump. During your next tennis practice, after warming up, try a lunge (reach forward with one leg, keeping the back leg stationary) as if you were reaching for a wide volley. If you feel tightness in the back of your thigh, your flexibility is probably not great enough to effectively make this shot without potential injury. If not properly stretched, the hamstring can be easily strained or injured by the fast movements in tennis.

Procedure

1. Lie on a table with a partner stabilizing your pelvis by holding down your hip bone.
2. Raise one leg until you feel tightness in the back of the leg. Keep your knee straight.
3. Your partner measures the angle at your hip with a goniometer (figure 3.2).
4. Repeat with the other leg.
5. Compare your scores with those listed in table 3.2.

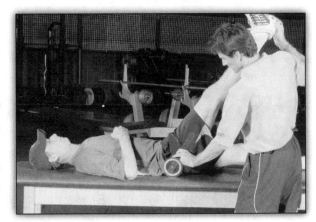

Figure 3.2

Table 3.2   Hamstring Flexibility (in degrees)

	Female	Male
Excellent	>85	>80
Good	75–85	70–80
Needs improvement	<75	<70

Hip Rotation

This test is also called Patrick's test or the FABER test, which stands for flexion, abduction, and external rotation of the hip.

Note: This test should be administered by a trained professional such as a physical therapist or athletic trainer.

A lack of hip rotation decreases a player's ability to generate maximal force from the lower extremities and transfer that force to provide power during tennis strokes. The hip rotator muscles are important stabilizers of the hip joint and can become very tight because of the multidirectional movements and stopping and starting inherent in tennis play. Reducing the tightness of these muscles helps to prevent hip injury and improve overall hip motion on court.

Procedure

1. Lie on your back on a treatment table.
2. With a pen, a qualified therapist or trainer marks the outside edge of the patella (knee cap) on each leg.
3. The examiner passively flexes, abducts, and externally rotates the hip of one leg by placing the ankle of that leg just above the patella of the leg that remains extended on the treatment table.

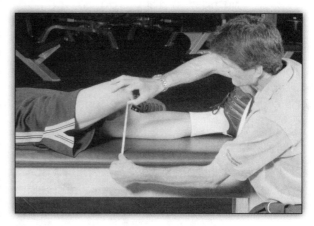

4. Relax your hip, and the examiner will measure the distance between the outside edge of the patella and the treatment table (figure 3.3).
5. Repeat the sequence on the other leg.
6. The examiner will expect to see bilateral symmetry between the lower extremities.

Figure 3.3

Note: Recent research has shown that tennis players should possess equal range of motion (flexibility) in both hips to maximize their performance.

Quadriceps Flexibility

Note: This test should be administered by a trained professional such as a physical therapist or athletic trainer.

The quadriceps is the large muscle in the front of the thigh. It is responsible for straightening your knee and flexing your hip. Quadriceps flexibility is important for decreasing the risk of knee injury and improving lower-body range of motion.

Procedure

1. Lie facedown on a treatment table with both legs straight.

2. A qualified examiner bends the knee of the testing leg to bring the heel toward the buttocks. Adequate flexibility requires the heel to touch the buttocks. If the examiner cannot touch the heel to the buttocks, use a goniometer to measure the knee angle achieved during the test (figure 3.4). Record this number to track progress and compare one leg to the other.

3. Perform the test on both legs. Both sides should be equal.

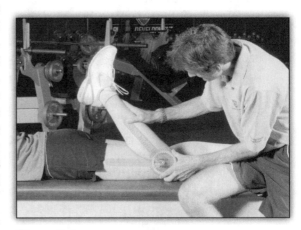

Figure 3.4

DVD Shoulder Flexibility Test

Note: This test should be administered by a trained professional such as a physical therapist or athletic trainer.

Shoulder flexibility determines how far you can move your arm around your shoulder joint. Adequate range of motion, both internal and external, is essential to injury prevention and good technique during strokes. With your upper arm at a 90-degree angle to your upper body (abduction), internal rotation brings your hand down so that the fingers point toward your toes. External rotation returns the hand upward so that your fingers point above your head. In neutral rotation, your fingers point directly toward the ceiling. If the internal or external rotator muscles are tighter than they should be, imbalances and shoulder injuries are more likely to occur. Many tennis players have poor internal rotation flexibility.

Procedure

1. Lie faceup (supine) on a treatment table. A qualified examiner will stabilize your scapula during testing to ensure that an accurate measurement is taken.

2. Position the upper arm at a 90-degree angle to the upper body (abduction). It remains in this position during the test. Bend the elbow at a 90-degree angle so that the fingers point toward the ceiling. This is the neutral position.

3. The examiner will ask you to rotate your shoulder internally (figure 3.5a) and externally (figure 3.5b) while the scapula remains stabilized and will record the maximum angle of movement with a goniometer.

4. Repeat with the other arm.

5. Compare your scores. A normal range of motion for the dominant arm is 150 degrees plus or minus 10 degrees. A normal range of motion for the nondominant arm is 160 degrees plus or minus 10 degrees.

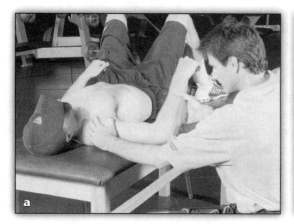 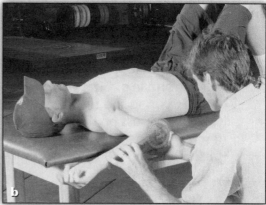

Figure 3.5

STRENGTH AND MUSCULAR ENDURANCE

Strength is the amount of weight you can lift or handle at any one time. Muscular endurance is the number of times your muscles can lift a weight or the length of time your muscles can hold an amount of weight. Not only is it important for tennis players to test their muscular strength but they also should test their muscular endurance because of the length of many tennis matches and the long hours of training and practice required to achieve elite levels of performance.

Have you ever played in a long match that made your muscles sore the next day? That's because tennis requires you to have not only good strokes but also strength and muscular endurance. Throughout a match, you may have to hit hundreds of balls while running from side to side. Good muscular endurance, which means that you can apply force and sustain it over time, can help you hit the ball just as hard at the end of a match as at the beginning. Not only that, it can also help prevent injuries.

STRENGTH AND MUSCULAR ENDURANCE TESTING

Sit-Up

We all know that strong legs are important for helping you get around the court as quickly as possible and that a strong arm is needed for a forceful swing. Equally important may be your abdominal and lower-back muscles. These muscles serve as an important link between the lower body and upper body as force is transferred from the ground all the way up to the racket. Studies have shown that these muscles contract intensely during most tennis strokes. For training purposes, you may want to perform crunches to reduce the strain on your hip flexors and lower back. However, for testing purposes, have someone hold your feet while you perform a complete Sit-Up. During testing, using an exercise that uses a full range of motion provides an easier way to measure how many Sit-Ups you perform in a certain time interval. Bending the trunk beyond 45 to 60 degrees during the Sit-Up causes a significant amount of hip flexor activity and relies less on the abdominal muscles for movement. The exercises described in chapter 7 are recommended for training, but the full Sit-Up is used during testing of abdominal power and endurance.

Procedure

1. Lie on your back with your knees bent and feet flat on the floor.
2. Have a partner hold your feet so they don't move while you perform the exercise.
3. Cross your arms over your chest and place your hands on opposite shoulders (figure 3.6).

Figure 3.6

4. Perform as many repetitions as you can in 60 seconds. Have your partner count and keep an eye on the clock.

5. To count as a complete Sit-Up, the elbows must touch the knees in the up position (while keeping the arms against the body), and the shoulder blades must touch the floor in the down position (hips must stay in contact with the floor).

6. Compare your scores with those listed in table 3.3.

Table 3.3 Sit-Ups Completed in 1 Minute

	Female		Male	
	Adult	Junior	Adult	Junior
Excellent	>53	>54	>58	>63
Good	46–53	46–54	51–58	56–63
Average	42–46	35–46	47–51	50–56
Needs improvement	<42	<35	<47	<50

Note: Players with a history of lower-back pain may need to refrain from performing this test.

Core Stability

Note: This test should be administered by a trained professional such as a physical therapist or athletic trainer.

One of the most important areas for all tennis players to train is the core of the body. This is generally described as the abdominals, lower back, and pelvis and consists of many muscle groups that are responsible for stabilizing the spine and transferring forces from the lower body to the upper body during virtually all sport activities and movement patterns. Chapter 7 covers the core extensively with exercises to improve core stability for tennis players.

Procedure

1. Lie on your back with your hips flexed 45 degrees and knees bent 90 degrees. Find a neutral spine position. A neutral spine position is one in which the body's normal curvature is maintained. The examiner will help determine the neutral spine position for the athlete to maintain during this test.

2. A qualified examiner places a blood pressure cuff under your lower back and inflates it so that you can maintain a level of 40 millimeters of mercury (mmHg) during a contraction of the transversus abdominis.

3. The examiner positions you in 90 degrees of hip and knee flexion and has you engage the transverse abdominus muscles to a level of 40 mmHg (figure 3.7).

4. Perform active movements, including alternately extending one knee and holding the extended leg for up to 10 seconds with the foot 15 centimeters above the ground. Repeat this movement alternately several times while maintaining

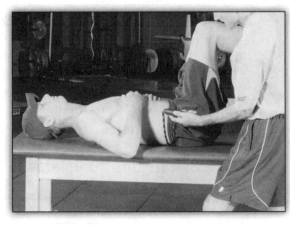

Figure 3.7

the pressure on the blood pressure cuff at 40 mmHg throughout the sets. The examiner can ensure that the appropriate muscles are engaged by feeling your abdomen to make sure the muscles are taut.

The inability to perform multiple leg extensions while maintaining 40 mmHg in the blood pressure cuff indicates the need for core stability training. This testing technique can also be used as a training exercise. The blood pressure cuff provides excellent feedback on your ability to contract the core musculature.

Push-Up

Do you want to hit your serve as hard as Andy Roddick does? Performing a Push-Up may not guarantee that you'll be able to serve 135 miles (217 kilometers) an hour; however, having strong shoulders and arms can certainly help you hit the ball harder and also reduce your risk of injury. A Push-Up is not necessarily a tennis-specific movement unless you fall down a lot and find yourself having to push yourself up off the ground. However, it does provide a good estimate of gross upper-body strength and muscle endurance and therefore has been used in many testing protocols for years. If doing a full Push-Up is too difficult, start by doing it against the wall, then progress to a modified Push-Up from your knees. Exercises like the Step-Up (page 181) are effective substitutes for the Push-Up for tennis players and place less stress on the shoulder joint, which prevents injury.

Procedure

1. Lie facedown with your hands shoulder-width apart.

2. Extend your arms, but keep your head, shoulders, back, hips, knees, and feet in a straight line. Support the weight of your lower body on your toes (figure 3.8).

3. Have a partner record the number of Push-Ups you complete in 60 seconds or to muscle failure.

4. To count as a complete Push-Up, the upper arm must reach parallel to the floor or below in the down position, the arms must be completely extended in the up position, and straight body alignment must be maintained.

5. Compare your scores with the ranges listed in table 3.4.

Figure 3.8

Table 3.4 Push-Ups Completed in 1 Minute

	Female		Male	
	Adult	Junior	Adult	Junior
Excellent	>44	>42	>49	>52
Good	36–44	34–42	40–49	49–52
Average	24–36	20–34	30–40	35–49
Needs improvement	<24	<20	<30	<35

Shoulder External Rotation Manual Muscle Test

Note: This test should be administered by a trained professional such as a physical therapist or athletic trainer.

The rotator cuff is responsible for stabilizing the shoulder during virtually all arm movements. Strength and muscular endurance in the external rotator muscles (back part of the rotator cuff) are essential for preventing shoulder injury. This test manually assesses the strength of the rotator cuff.

Procedure

1. You may sit or stand. A qualified examiner places your shoulder in 90 degrees of abduction and 90 degrees of external rotation in the coronal plane (90/90 position). The elbow is bent 90 degrees.

2. While using one arm to stabilize your elbow, the examiner exerts a force into internal rotation (figure 3.9). You should attempt to hold the initial 90/90 position.

3. The examiner grades and records the performance of both arms based on the following scale:

Figure 3.9

5 (normal): ability to maintain the 90/90 position without pain against maximal resistance by the examiner. The arm does not break from the 90/90 position with testing.

4 (good): ability to maintain 90/90 position without pain against moderate resistance exerted by the examiner. The hand and forearm move slightly into internal rotation with stronger resistance applied by the examiner.

3 (fair): inability to withstand any resistance applied by the examiner.

2 (poor): inability to place the arm in the 90/90 position.

4. Record the score as a ratio based on 5/5 as normal. A score less than 5/5 indicates the need for rotator cuff and scapular strengthening.

Note: Additional testing can be performed using isokinetic machines to more accurately test the internal and external rotators of the shoulder. Test with 90 degrees of abduction. (See Ellenbecker and Roetert, *Journal of Science and Medicine in Sport,* 2003, Mar. 6(1): 63-70.) Research has shown that elite-level tennis players have equal external rotation strength in their dominant and nondominant arms, but 20 to 30 percent greater internal rotation strength in their dominant arms.

Scapular Stabilization

Note: This test should be administered by a trained professional such as a physical therapist or athletic trainer.

The shoulder blade or scapula is the base for arm movement and an anchor for muscular attachment. The scapula must line up and move with the arm like a ball on a seal's nose. Although tennis players have extraordinary strength in some areas, they often lack proper strength and development of the muscles in the upper back. This test checks for scapular motion and control of that motion.

Procedure

1. Stand and hold a 1-pound (0.45-kilogram) weight in each hand.

2. Begin with your arms at your sides. When directed by a qualified instructor, elevate or raise your straight arms for multiple repetitions (figure 3.10).

3. A qualified examiner observes the movement of the scapula and notes any

Figure 3.10

winging (protrusion of the scapula away from the back) or overuse of the neck and upper-trapezius muscles during both the ascent and descent. The examiner watches scapular motion and notes any asymmetry. This is especially important as the arms come down.

One-Leg Stability Test

This test indicates a player's ability to control the body over the planted leg. This is important for decreasing loads on the knee and leg, which decreases the risk of injury, and for allowing explosive starts and stops, which enhance performance. It is an excellent test for identifying weaknesses of the core, hip, and knee. It also is an important screening tool for determining a player's ability to balance. Careful observation of the player's movement strategies can provide important information for training and injury prevention.

Procedure

1. Stand with your arms at your sides. You can bend your non-weight-bearing knee to as much as 90 degrees (figure 3.11*a*).

2. Look forward and bend the weight-bearing knee approximately 30 degrees (partial squat) (figure 3.11*b*).

3. Repeat several times on both legs.

Figure 3.11

4. A qualified examiner looks for several compensations during the test, including an inability to control the pelvis (Trendelenburg's sign), corkscrewing, and the use of excessive trunk flexion during the descent. The examiner should also note the inability to maintain proper balance throughout the test.

Grip Strength

Adequate grip strength can help prevent wrist and elbow injuries. In addition, it can help you hold on to your racket more securely on off-center hits. Although your dominant arm will be stronger than your nondominant arm, professionals recommend that the difference between the two should not be greater than 25 percent. Grip strength measures the strength of the finger flexors and forearm muscles.

Procedure

1. Hold your arm at your side and squeeze a grip-strength dynamometer (figure 3.12).
2. Record the result in kilograms (1 kilogram is 2.2 pounds).
3. Repeat on other side.
4. Compare your scores with the ranges in table 3.5.

Figure 3.12

Table 3.5   Grip Strength (in kilograms)

	Female		Male	
	Adult	**Junior**	**Adult**	**Junior**
Excellent				
Dominant	>39	>37	>60	>52
Nondominant	>27	>33	>36	>42
Good				
Dominant	34–39	34–37	51–60	48–52
Nondominant	24–27	27–33	31–36	34–42
Average				
Dominant	28–34	31–34	42–51	39–48
Nondominant	22–24	25–27	26–31	31–34
Needs improvement				
Dominant	<28	<31	<42	<39
Nondominant	<22	<25	<26	<31

POWER

Power is the amount of work you can perform in a given period. Power is required for activities that rely on both strength and speed.

Tennis requires you to move explosively. Greater power allows you to respond more quickly and produce more forceful movements with less effort. Players with explosive first steps get into position quickly, set up well, and hit effective shots. In addition, an explosive first step gives you the speed to get to balls hit farther away. Both upper- and lower-body power are necessary in tennis. To maximize your power, your lower-body power must be transferred to the upper body.

POWER TESTING

Vertical Jump

Everybody is born with a certain amount of athletic ability; however, you can improve your vertical jump and lower-body power. Power is a combination of muscular strength and movement speed. Training the lower body means developing an explosive first step. As mentioned previously,

research shows that during an average 5-second point in a tennis match, there can be as many as four direction changes. Therefore, it is important to develop powerful legs. The vertical jump is a measure of lower-body power. It is the height you can reach while jumping from a standing position minus the height you can reach when standing.

Procedure: Vertical jump can be measured using one of several pieces of equipment designed for this purpose.

1. After adjusting the height of the device, reach up with both hands, keeping your heels on the ground, to establish your reach height.

2. Jump as high as you can, hitting the vanes of the measuring device with your hand (figure 3.13).

3. Perform at least two jumps, but continue until you do not hit any additional vanes.

Figure 3.13

Vertical jump can also be measured without any special equipment.

1. Stand with your side to a wall. Reach up and touch the wall as high as you can.
2. Have a partner mark the spot you touch on the wall.
3. Attach a measuring stick to the wall from the highest reach of your fingertips.
4. Put chalk on your fingers.
5. Jump with your side to the wall (do not take a step), reaching as high as you can on the measuring stick.
6. The difference between your standing reach and the highest point of your jump is your score.
7. Compare your scores with the ranges in table 3.6.

Table 3.6　Vertical Jump (in inches*)

	Female		Male	
	Adult	**Junior**	**Adult**	**Junior**
Excellent	>21	>22	>27	>28
Good	16–21	17–22	22–27	26–28
Average	12–16	13–17	17–22	21–26
Needs improvement	<12	<13	<17	<21

*1 inch = 2.5 centimeters

Note: In addition to the vertical jump to estimate lower-body power, a physical therapist or athletic trainer can perform a test on an isokinetic machine to measure the strength of your thigh muscles (quadriceps and hamstrings). In addition to comparing your left and right legs and determining if strength deficiencies are present, the machine allows for comparison between muscles groups to gauge if you have proper muscle balance. Research has shown that tennis players have equally strong quadriceps and hamstring muscles in both legs. Additionally, research has shown that disproportionate muscle balance between the hamstrings and quadriceps can lead to knee injury and poor performance.

DVD Medicine Ball Toss, Forehand and Backhand

Training with a medicine ball can be practical because you can mimic tennis strokes. Tossing the medicine ball involves the whole body, or kinetic chain. Research has shown a strong relationship between performing well in these tests and overall fitness in tennis players. Pay particular attention to the tossing technique. Proper technique will involve knee flexion and extension and a significant amount of trunk rotation, not just a toss with the arms.

Procedure

1. Stand at a designated spot facing forward and hold a 6-pound (2.7-kilogram) medicine ball.

2. Take one step and toss the ball, simulating a forehand stroke, while staying behind the starting line (figure 3.14).

3. Measure the distance from the line to the point where the ball lands.

4. Repeat for the backhand side (figure 3.15).

5. Compare your scores with the ranges in tables 3.7 and 3.8.

Figure 3.14

Figure 3.15

Table 3.7 Forehand Medicine Ball Toss (in feet*)

	Female		Male	
	Adult	Junior	Adult	Junior
Excellent	>30.5	>32	>39	>42
Good	25–30.5	26–32	32–39	35–42
Average	19.5–25	20–26	25–32	28–35
Needs improvement	<19.5	<20	<25	<28

*1 foot = 30.5 centimeters

Table 3.8 Backhand Medicine Ball Toss (in feet*)

	Female		Male	
	Adult	Junior	Adult	Junior
Excellent	>30	>31	>37.5	>42
Good	24–30	25–31	30.5–37.5	34–42
Average	17.5–24	18–25	23.5–30.5	26–34
Needs improvement	<17.5	<18	<23.5	<26

*1 foot = 30.5 centimeters

DVD Medicine Ball Toss, Overhead and Reverse Overhead

The overhead and reverse overhead tosses use the same muscle groups as those used in the serve and overhead. You will be most successful if you use ground reaction forces properly. Remember the principle from physics class, "For every action there is an equal and opposite reaction." Releasing the medicine ball at an approximately 45-degree angle will give you the best results.

Procedure

1. Stand facing forward behind a line and hold a 6-pound (2.7-kilogram) medicine ball.

2. Toss the ball from an overhead position as far as possible using only one step (figure 3.16). Do not cross the line.

3. Measure the distance from the line to the point where the ball lands.

4. Repeat the procedure for a reverse overhead toss (figure 3.17). Take no step on this toss.

5. Compare your scores with the ranges in tables 3.9 and 3.10.

Figure 3.16

Figure 3.17

Table 3.9 Overhead Medicine Ball Toss (in feet*)

	Female		Male	
	Adult	Junior	Adult	Junior
Excellent	>22.5	>23	>30.5	>34
Good	18.5–22.5	19–23	25.5–30.5	29–34
Average	14.5–18.5	15–19	20–25.5	23–29
Needs improvement	<14.5	<15	<20	<23

*1 foot = 30.5 centimeters

Table 3.10　Reverse Medicine Ball Toss (in feet*)

	Female		Male	
	Adult	Junior	Adult	Junior
Excellent	>32.5	>34	>43.5	>46
Good	26.5–32.5	27–34	35–43.5	38–46
Average	20.5–26.5	20–27	27–35	31–38
Needs improvement	<20.5	<20	<27	<31

*1 foot = 30.5 centimeters

AGILITY AND SPEED

Agility and speed describe the ability to move around the court quickly and smoothly to position yourself for a shot. Agility is crucial to good court movement. It allows you to be in the correct position and provides a solid platform from which to hit the ball. Speed is important for getting to the ball. Although some people have natural speed, other athletes can improve speed by training their muscles and nervous systems to produce the same effect. The faster you can get to a ball, the more time you have to prepare for your shot.

AGILITY AND SPEED TESTING

Hexagon Test

This test measures foot quickness when changing direction backward, forward, and sideways while facing in one direction. Facing in the same direction during the test simulates facing your opponent during a match. The Hexagon also tests your ability to stabilize the body quickly between changes of direction because the body needs to be stable before you can perform the next jump. If the body is not stable, you will lose your balance.

Procedure

1. Use masking tape to create a hexagon on the ground (six sides with angles of 120 degrees). Make sure all six sides are 24 inches (61 centimeters) long (figure 3.18).
2. Stand in the middle of the hexagon and remain facing in the same direction throughout the test.
3. When your partner gives you the command "ready, go," begin jumping forward over the tape and immediately back into the hexagon.

Your partner will time you with a stopwatch.

4. Continuing to face forward, jump over the next side and back to the middle. Repeat for each side.

5. Continue this pattern by jumping over all six sides and back to the middle each time for three full revolutions of the hexagon.

6. When the feet enter the hexagon after three full revolutions, your partner should stop the watch and record your time.

7. Give yourself one practice trial. Test yourself twice, recording both times with the stopwatch. Make a note of your best time.

8. Compare your scores with the ranges in table 3.11.

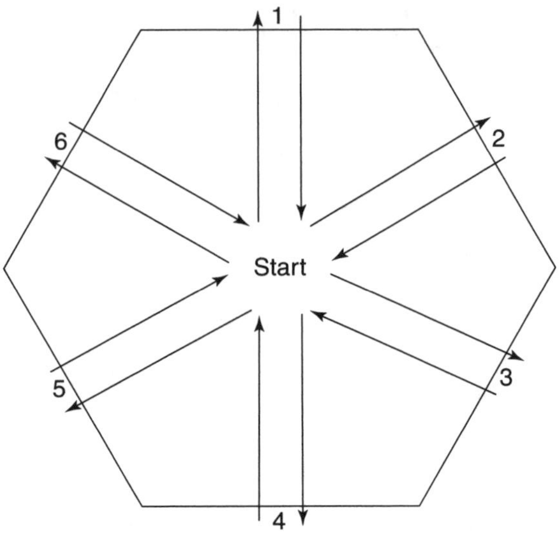

Figure 3.18

Table 3.11 Hexagon (in seconds)

	Female		Male	
	Adult	**Junior**	**Adult**	**Junior**
Excellent	<12.00	<10.48	<11.80	<11.10
Good	12.00–12.10	10.48–11.70	11.80–13.00	11.10–11.80
Average	12.10–12.40	11.70–12.30	13.00–13.50	11.80–12.70
Needs improvement	>12.40	>12.30	>13.50	>12.70

20-Yard Dash

Roger Federer and Justine Henin are two of the fastest players in professional tennis. It's no wonder they're also at the top of the rankings. You can't hit a good shot if you don't have enough time to get in position. Sport science research shows us that an average point in tennis lasts 5 to 10 seconds. Therefore, explosive speed is important.

Procedure

1. Mark off 20 yards (18.2 meters) on a tennis court with masking tape. The distance from the baseline to the opposite side service line is 20 yards.

2. Have a partner stand at the finish line with an arm in the air and stopwatch in hand.

3. At the drop of the arm and the command "ready, go," sprint toward the finish line.

4. Complete three trials. Record the best of the three scores.

5. Compare your score with the ranges in table 3.12.

Table 3.12 20-Yard* Dash (in seconds)

	Female		Male	
	Adult	**Junior**	**Adult**	**Junior**
Excellent	<3.30	<3.20	<3.20	<2.90
Good	3.30–3.40	3.20–3.36	3.20–3.30	2.90–3.00
Average	3.40–3.60	3.36–3.54	3.30–3.50	3.00–3.30
Needs improvement	>3.60	>3.54	>3.50	>3.30

*20 yards equals 18.2 meters.

Spider Run Test

DVD

Remember the old shuttle run in school? Well, the Spider Run is tennis' version of the shuttle run. Of all the physical fitness tests we administer to players, the movement patterns in this test most closely simulate the actual movements during a tennis match. The stopping and starting actions of this activity make it an excellent test as well as a great training drill.

Procedure

1. Using masking tape, mark off a 12-by-18-inch (30-by-46-centimeter) rectangle behind the center of the baseline, using the baseline as one of the sides.

2. Position five tennis balls on the court—one on each corner where the baseline and singles sideline meet, one on each side where the singles sideline and service line meet, and one ball on the T (figure 3.19).

3. Start with one foot in the rectangle. Retrieve each ball and place it in the rectangle, one at a time, moving in a counterclockwise direction.

4. Have a partner record your time with a stopwatch. As soon as you place the last ball in the rectangle, your partner stops the watch.

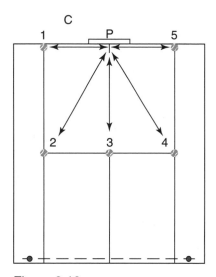

Figure 3.19

5. Compare your score with the ranges in table 3.13.

Table 3.13 Spider Run (in seconds)

	Female		Male	
	Adult	**Junior**	**Adult**	**Junior**
Excellent	<17.30	<17.10	<15.00	<14.60
Good	17.30–18.00	17.10–17.16	15.00–15.30	14.60–15.00
Average	18.00–18.30	17.16–17.34	15.30–16.00	15.00–15.40
Needs improvement	>18.30	>17.34	>16.00	>15.40

Sideways Shuffle

The Sideways Shuffle is a speed and agility test that focuses on lateral movement. Many speed and agility tests measure forward speed; however, lateral speed is just as important in tennis. Much of your time on the baseline is spent shuffling from side to side, retrieving forehands and backhands. Moving quickly while staying balanced (keeping your center of gravity over your base of support) is critical in this exercise.

Procedure

1. Start on the center service line at the T with one foot on either side of the line, facing the net.
2. While facing the net, shuffle along the service line and touch the doubles sideline with your foot. Then shuffle to the opposite doubles sideline and continue back to the center. Crossover steps are not allowed.
3. Have a partner record your time with a stopwatch. After you touch both doubles sidelines and return to the center, your partner stops the watch.
4. Compare your score with the ranges in table 3.14.

Table 3.14 Sideways Shuffle (in seconds)

	Female		Male	
	Adult	**Junior**	**Adult**	**Junior**
Excellent	<6.0	<7.0	<6.4	<5.5
Good	6.0–7.0	7.0–7.1	6.4–6.7	5.5–5.6
Average	7.0–7.3	7.1–7.4	6.7–7.0	5.6–5.7
Needs improvement	>7.3	>7.4	>7.0	>5.7

BODY COMPOSITION

Body composition refers to the approximate percentages of fat, muscle, bone, and water that make up your body. It can be measured through various methods. Percent body fat gives a good indication of your physical condition.

The amount of bone and water that your body is composed of remains constant, so pay attention to muscle and fat when attempting to alter body composition. You can increase the amount of muscle in the body through proper strength training. However, it is not enough to just increase muscle mass; you must also work to maintain an appropriate level of body fat.

The two ways to affect body fat are fat-loss dieting and aerobic exercise. Fat-loss dieting, which is the appropriate term for a weight-loss diet because you are attempting to decrease fat in particular, is a method of decreasing fat intake while maintaining an adequate caloric intake. Along with using fat as an energy source, aerobic exercise will also improve endurance in longer matches. Body fat percentages to shoot for are 8 to 18 percent for men and 15 to 25 percent for women. By following a balanced diet and including aerobic exercise (a few sets of tennis) in your training regimen, these percentages will be an attainable goal.

BODY COMPOSITION TESTING

Skinfold

Caution: This test should be administered by a trained professional.

Skinfold measurements provide a relatively simple and noninvasive method of estimating general body composition. Measurements are taken at three sites and the sum is entered into an equation for the prediction of body composition.

Procedure

1. The sites measured on men are the chest, abdomen, and thigh. The sites measured on women are the triceps, suprailium, and thigh.
2. Have a qualified professional measure the skinfolds at three sites on your body.
3. Add the sum of the three skinfold measurements and compare your percentage to the ranges for your gender (8 to 18 percent for men; 15 to 25 percent for women).

AEROBIC ENDURANCE

Aerobic endurance is the ability to take in, transport, and use oxygen. Aerobic energy is used during prolonged, steady-paced activities that mainly use the large muscle groups. Examples include jogging, cycling, and swimming.

Aerobic endurance is important in tennis. When you are aerobically fit, you can recover faster between points and perform longer before getting tired. A strong aerobic base allows you to recover efficiently between points even during long, close matches. As your endurance improves, your ligaments and tendons will become tougher, reducing the risk of injury and laying the foundation for more intense training.

AEROBIC ENDURANCE TESTING

1.5-Mile Run

Although tennis involves many short sprints on the court, there is also an aerobic endurance component. Matches can last 3 hours or longer, taxing the aerobic system. When completing the 1.5-mile (2.4-kilometer) distance, you should focus on running at a consistent pace throughout the run. Training for longer distances should be done mostly in the off-season and preseason.

It's important to be consistent when testing and retesting. If possible, retest on the same track as used for the initial test. Many tracks in the United States are now 400 meters per lap, so it will take slightly more than six laps to complete 1.5 miles.

Procedure

1. Stand on a level track.
2. A partner gives the command "ready, go" and starts a stopwatch.
3. Complete 1.5 miles (2.4 kilometers) and record your time.
4. Compare your score with the times in table 3.15.

Table 3.15   1.5-Mile Run (in minutes:seconds)

	Female		Male	
	Adult	**Junior**	**Adult**	**Junior**
Excellent	<11:49	<10:30	<8:44	<9:45
Good	11:49–13:43	10:30–11:00	8:44–10:47	9:45–10:15
Average	13:43–15:08	11:00–11:30	10:47–12:20	10:15–11:00
Needs improvement	>15:08	>11:30	>12:20	>11:00

Note: Another test that can be performed by an exercise physiologist in an exercise laboratory is a $\dot{V}O_2$max test. Using a progressive series of exercise stages on a treadmill or cycle ergometer, this test measures the maximum amount of oxygen that a player can use. This test can provide an excellent measure of aerobic fitness to identify players with either exceptional aerobic capacity or players who may need to further emphasize aerobic exercise in their off-court training programs.

SUMMARY

The tests described in this chapter can be used to provide tennis players with critical indicators of athletic performance as well as specific measures of strength, power, flexibility, and endurance. Perform these tests before developing a complete conditioning program in order to identify strengths and weaknesses and enable each player's program to be individually designed to maximize effectiveness. In most cases, repeating the tests more frequently than 6 to 8 weeks will not show significant changes because the human performance variables measured in these tests take time to develop. However, testing should occur at regular intervals to gauge improvement and allow for adjustments to the player's training regimen. Following injury, more frequent testing can be applied in order to closely monitor the player's progress and development. Use of the normative data provided in this chapter can quickly determine how a player stacks up against the large groups of players we have tested; however, the most valuable testing comparisons are between testing sessions in which a player's improvement can be monitored and measured.

Chapter 4

Dynamic Warm-Up and Flexibility

A high-quality conditioning program for tennis includes strength, flexibility, and anaerobic and aerobic training. If tennis players neglect a component in their training program, they are unlikely to achieve their full performance potential and are more susceptible to injury while playing. Recent changes in the understanding of flexibility exercises have identified the critical need for warm-up and dynamic stretching before tennis play and high-level physical performance. Understanding the essential components of a proper warm-up and the differences between static stretching and dynamic stretching is important to optimizing performance and at the same time minimizing injury risk.

The physical demands of playing tennis stress all regions of the body and as such, proper warm-up and flexibility training must include all areas of the body. Injuries to the upper and lower extremities as well as the spine and torso have been reported in elite and recreational players and will be discussed later in chapter 12.

WARM-UP

The warm-up plays an important part in a tennis player's conditioning program. Warm-up exercises should be performed before flexibility work. The purposes of the warm-up are to prepare the body tissues to optimally respond to the exercises and stretches applied during the workout and to prevent injury.

Athletes often use two types of warm-ups. A passive warm-up involves the application of an external source of heat to the body. Examples of passive warm-up methods include applying moist heat packs and heating pads and using a warm whirlpool before exercise. These techniques increase tissue temperature but are not always practical for most athletes. A second type of warm-up is the active warm-up. An active warm-up involves low-intensity exercise that elevates tissue temperature, increases heart rate, and actively prepares the athlete for exercise.

Recommended activities for an active warm-up are Jumping Jacks, calisthenics, slow jogging or jogging in place, low-intensity stationary cycling, and large arm circles (clockwise and counterclockwise).

A good indicator that the duration and intensity of the warm-up are appropriate is the presence of a light sweat. Using the recommended active warm-up exercises, this is often achieved in 3 to 5 minutes. Additional benefits of a proper warm-up are improved tissue elasticity and a reduced risk of muscle and tendon injury.

FLEXIBILITY TRAINING

Flexibility training is often the most overlooked and least adhered to component of a conditioning program. Some of the reasons for this include the following:

- Stretching doesn't feel particularly good.
- Stetching's on-court benefits are not obvious to the player.
- Most players have not received individualized guidelines for how, why, what, and when to stretch.
- Many coaches give stretching less emphasis than they give other components of conditioning.

Flexibility can be defined as the degree of extensibility of the soft tissue structures, such as muscles, tendons, and connective tissue, that surround the joint. There are several types of flexibility. Static flexibility describes the measured range of motion about a joint or series of joints. Dynamic flexibility refers to the active motion around a joint or series of joints. Dynamic flexibility is limited by the joint structure's resistance to motion, the ability of the soft connective tissues to deform, and the neuromuscular components.

Factors influencing flexibility include heredity, neuromuscular components, and tissue temperature. In regard to heredity, body design determines overall flexibility potential. Although most people tend to be relatively inflexible, some are "loose jointed," or hyperflexible. Aspects of heredity and body design that affect our flexibility potential include the shape and orientation of joint surfaces, as well as the physiological characteristics of the joint capsule, muscles, tendons, and ligaments. Additionally, because of the nature of the movements performed while playing tennis and from the repetitive nature of these stresses, some areas of the tennis player's body, such as the hamstrings, lower back, and muscles in the back of the shoulder, can be very tight and inflexible, while other areas, like the front of the shoulder (which allows for external rotation), may be very loose and overly flexible.

Few people are as flexible around their joints as they need to be, and tennis play places tremendous demands on the body parts that experience extremes of motion. For example, the range of motion required of the shoulder as it externally rotates during the serve places tremendous stress on the front of the shoulder. Tennis players generally are very flexible in external rotation of the shoulder but exhibit limited internal rotation on their dominant (tennis-playing) side. To demonstrate this, try this simple test. Place the back surface of both hands with the thumbs pointing up in the lower back and reach up toward the shoulder blades as high as possible. Notice that your dominant arm is not likely to reach as high as the nondominant arm. This shows the loss of internal shoulder rotation that is common in elite tennis players and also in other types of throwing athletes. The stretches outlined for the posterior (back) part of the shoulder later in this chapter should enhance the range of motion for this joint and decrease the difference between the two sides. To address this flexibility imbalance, specific stretches for the back of the shoulder are recommended, and exercises that stress the front of the shoulder by placing the arms behind the body (such as in a doorway) are not recommended for tennis players and throwing athletes. Figure 4.1 depicts the human muscular system for reference when designing your flexibility program.

Additional examples of extreme ranges of motion common during tennis play include the following:

- Lateral movement patterns that stress the hip and groin
- Stabilizing muscle actions of the abdominal muscles during the tennis serve
- Explosive movement patterns by the calf muscles and Achilles tendon

Throughout a match, players have to generate great force and speed while in an outstretched position. A conditioning program that includes flexibility exercises ensures that the range of motion necessary for optimal performance will be available. It is important to note that flexibility, combined with the ability to produce power in these extremes of motion, is essential in tennis. Stretching alone will not prevent injury or enhance performance; however, balanced strength throughout a flexible, less restricted range of motion will. This goal can only be attained using a complete conditioning program for tennis.

Flexibility offers the following benefits:

- Provides the framework for strengthening muscles and joints that experience extreme motions
- Helps tissue distribute impact and force more effectively, thus allowing tissue to accommodate the stresses imposed on it
- Lessens the work of opposing muscle groups by providing more unrestricted motion

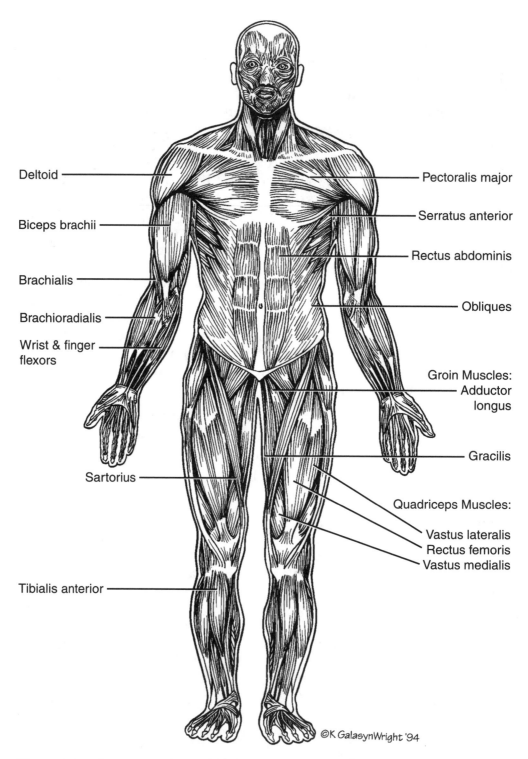

Deltoid

Biceps brachii

Brachialis

Brachioradialis

Wrist & finger
flexors

Sartorius

Tibialis anterior

Pectoralis major

Serratus anterior

Rectus abdominis

Obliques

Groin Muscles:
Adductor
longus

Gracilis

Quadriceps Muscles:

Vastus lateralis
Rectus femoris
Vastus medialis

©K GalasynWright '94

Figure 4.1a Front view of adult human skeletal musculature.
© K. Galasyn-Wright, Champaign, IL, 1994.

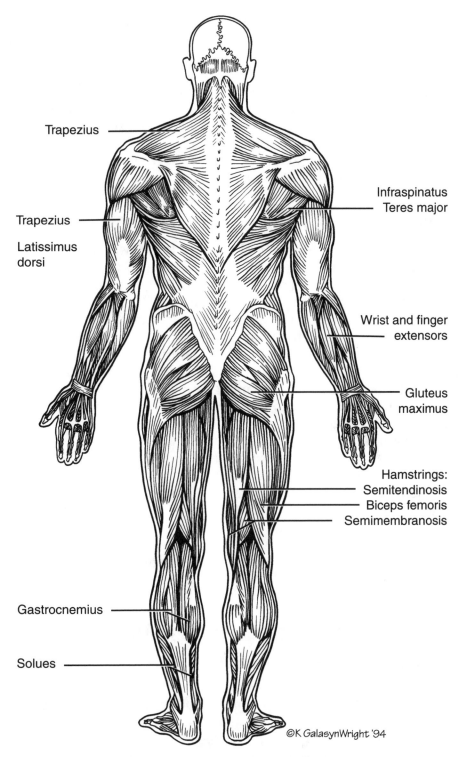

Trapezius

Trapezius

Latissimus
dorsi

Infraspinatus
Teres major

Wrist and finger
extensors

Gluteus
maximus

Hamstrings:
Semitendinosis
Biceps femoris
Semimembranosis

Gastrocnemius

Solues

©K GalasynWright '94

Figure 4.1*b*   Rear view of adult human skeletal musculature.

© K. Galasyn-Wright, Champaign, IL, 1994.

- Enhances blood supply and tissue nourishment
- Allows good form without compensation from other body segments
- Overcomes imbalances created by the sport and by daily activities

You may want to include more than one stretching exercise for body segments that have a more limited range of motion. Once you can perform one stretch, you may want to try a more advanced stretch for that area. Focus on the areas of the body that are the most inflexible. Stretching only the areas that are already flexible will take time from other areas that need special attention.

WARM-UP AND FLEXIBILITY ROUTINE

Major changes have occurred in the way athletes warm up and stretch before performing. The biggest change has been in the shift away from doing static stretches before playing or practicing and performing a more complete dynamic stretching or warm-up routine to optimally prepare the body's muscles, tendons, and joints for the stresses of physical activity.

Until recently, sport scientists and sports medicine professionals recommended static stretching before and after tennis play or any other type of vigorous exercise. The slow movements and periods of holding at or near the end of the range of motion characteristic of static stretching programs were found in several studies to provide optimal lengthening of the muscle tissues. Dynamic stretching and warm-up were mentioned but not necessarily emphasized in most workout routines.

However, recent research has identified temporary decreases in skeletal muscle performance immediately after static stretching. This decrease in muscle performance includes decreases in both muscular strength and power and can last for up to 1 hour after a static stretching program. Applying this research to athletes has led sport scientists and medical professionals to now recommend static stretching at least 30 minutes before the start of an activity such as tennis or training and to emphasize the importance of a dynamic warm-up immediately before tennis play, practice sessions,

INCORPORATING STRETCHING WITH TENNIS

1. Perform a general-body warm-up (3 to 5 minutes) to increase tissue temperature, possibly including a slow jog, Jumping Jacks, and so on.
2. Perform a dynamic stretching sequence, progressively increasing the range of motion and velocity of movement.
3. Play tennis or perform a vigorous workout.
4. During the cool-down, perform static stretching of the areas that are particularly tight to prevent muscle soreness and gain more flexibility.

and vigorous training sessions. Specifically, the use of a generous warm-up (jogging in place or riding a stationary bicycle for 3 to 5 minutes to break a light sweat) is now highly recommended along with dynamic stretches immediately before the activity is performed. Static stretching, although still important and still used, is now applied primarily after training and will be covered in greater detail later in this chapter. Static stretching after the workout is thought to speed recovery and decrease soreness in addition to increase muscle length. The sidebar Incorporating Stretching With Tennis summarizes the sequence for integrating a dynamic warm-up with tennis play or practice sessions and includes the integration of static stretching into the overall program for tennis players.

An important influence on flexibility involves the neuromuscular components. The muscle spindle is a watchdog mechanism, located between the muscle fibers. When a stretch is imposed on it too quickly, the muscle spindle sends a message to the central nervous system (CNS) to contract the muscle. With this stretch reflex, the muscle shortens, thus hindering the stretching process. Therefore, when stretching, a slow, gradual movement minimizes the reflex action of the muscle spindle mechanism and enhances the stretching process.

Another factor influencing flexibility and important during all stretching exercises is tissue temperature. Heat increases the extensibility of soft tissue. Warming up before stretching by raising the body's core temperature and breaking a light sweat will result in greater gains in flexibility, with less microtrauma to the tissues being stretched. Another benefit to the stretching sequence in this chapter is the emphasis on static stretching after exercise or tennis play. This is when the body is maximally warmed-up and accepting of a static-stretching program. Static stretching is one part of the flexibility training program that is most often overlooked or underused. In the flexibility sequence recommended in the sidebar (page 48), static stretching after exercise is important and helps the player improve muscle length, which can prevent injury and enhance performance.

Dynamic Stretching

The best recommendation for integrating a series of dynamic stretches into a training program is to always perform a proper warm-up first. The warm-up is one of the most important aspects of all types of stretching programs. Recommended warm-up activities include slow jogging around the court while making progressively larger arm circles, riding a bike, using a slide board, or performing any other rhythmic, aerobic-type activity. The warm-up should typically last 3 to 5 minutes, and occasionally more; however, you should perform these actions at very low intensities.

Once the player has warmed up enough to break a light sweat, he or she can perform several repetitions of dynamic stretching sequences, progressively increasing the intensity. The sidebar Dynamic Stretching Sequence for Tennis Players contains an example of an on-court sequence.

This program is typically performed with players moving back and forth across the width of the tennis court. One series of all 11 exercises is recommended for most players.

Recommended dynamic stretches include Butt Kick, Front Lunge, Side Lunge, Jogging With Arm Circles, and some tennis-specific stretches. Little guidance from the literature exists on how many repetitions of each stretch are optimal; however, each player most likely will have individual needs. Multiple repetitions of each movement are recommended. And more movements are encouraged to alleviate the stiffness caused by cooler temperatures, tournaments with frequent matches, and intense training sessions.

DYNAMIC STRETCHING SEQUENCE FOR TENNIS PLAYERS

A recommended series of dynamic warm-up activities is listed below. Performing each movement across the court and back provides an effective warm-up.

1. Walk or jog back and forth across the court while making progressively larger arm circles.
2. Cross the court by performing the Knee-to-Chest Tuck with one leg and rising up on the toes with the other leg. Alternate legs as you proceed across the court.
3. Perform the Figure-4 Tuck.
4. Perform the Side Lunge across the court. As you move across the court, step farther to stretch the muscles on the inside of the upper thigh (groin).
5. Perform the Frankenstein Walk.
6. Perform the High-Step Trunk Rotation. Increase the amount of trunk rotation and the height of your knee as you cross the court.
7. Perform the Front Lunge. Be sure to keep your torso upright as you move forward and don't let the knee extend past the toes.
8. Perform the Torso Rotation, progressing to Torso Rotation With Squat. You can do these in place.
9. Perform the Backward Lunge With Trunk Rotation. Reach with your arm to your opposite leg (for example, right leg back, rotate to the left, and reach with your left hand to your right ankle).
10. Perform the Butt Kick.
11. Perform Hug the World, Hug Yourself.

DYNAMIC STRETCHES

Jogging With Arm Circles

Focus: Improve the flexibility in the shoulders, chest, and upper back.

Procedure
1. Start at the doubles sideline facing across the court.
2. Swing the arms forward in large circles as you jog at a moderate pace from doubles sideline to doubles sideline.
3. Change directions and swing the arms in backward circles as you jog back to the start position.
4. Repeat one or two times across the court.

Side Step With Arm Crosses

Focus: Improve the flexibility in the shoulders, chest, and upper back.

Procedure
1. Start at the doubles sideline facing the net.
2. Lift the arms out to the sides to shoulder height while assuming an athletic stance (knees and hips slightly flexed with the torso relatively upright and facing forward).
3. While shuffling across the court using side-shuffle steps, swing your arms across your body like you are hugging yourself, and then swing the arms backward until you feel a slight stretch in the front of your shoulders and chest.
4. Perform this exercise as you shuffle from doubles sideline to doubles sideline, once to your left, and returning to your right.

Carioca

Focus: Improve the flexibility of the lower legs and trunk.

Procedure

1. Assume an athletic position while facing the net on the doubles sideline.
2. Begin by pushing off the right leg and stepping outward with the left foot toward the middle of the court. Upon landing on the left foot, cross the right foot in front of the left (figure 4.2).
3. Again push off the right foot, landing on the left. This time on landing, cross the right leg behind the left leg.
4. Repeat this cycle until you arrive at the doubles sideline. You will perform a repeating cycle of crosses with the right leg crossing in front of and then behind the left as you proceed across the court. Reverse directions while still facing the net and this time the left leg crosses in front of and behind the right leg as you return to the baseline you started from.

Figure 4.2

Knee-to-Chest Tuck

Focus: Improve the flexibility in the hips, trunk, and lower extremities.

Procedure

1. Stand on the doubles sideline facing across the court.
2. Bring one knee toward the chest. Hug the knee up tight toward you as you straighten your other knee and rise up on your toes (figure 4.3).
3. Take a small hop forward, landing on the same leg while returning the other leg from the chest down toward the ground.
4. Repeat, alternating each leg across the court and return to the starting position. Repeat once or twice across the court.

Figure 4.3

Knee-Hug Lunge

Focus: Improve the flexibility in the hips, trunk, and lower extremities; added benefit for hip flexors and quads.

Procedure

1. Stand on the doubles sideline facing across the court.

2. Bring one knee up toward the chest. Hug the knee up tight toward you as you straighten your other knee and rise up onto your toes (figure 4.4*a*).

3. Take a small hop forward, landing on the same leg while returning the other leg from the chest down toward the ground.

4. Immediately take a large step forward directly into a lunge (figure 4.4*b*). Hold this position for 1 to 2 seconds.

5. Stand up after holding the lunge, driving up with the front leg. Repeat the cycle as you proceed across the court.

Figure 4.4

DVD Inverted Hamstrings

Focus: Improve the flexibility and balance of the hamstrings and gluteals.

Procedure

1. Start at the doubles sideline, facing across the court.
2. Stand on one leg and bend forward at the waist. Keep the leg on the ground slightly bent.
3. Bend forward until you feel a stretch in the hamstrings of the leg on the ground. Keep the back flat and avoid twisting.
4. Elevate the raised leg behind, holding it in line with your body (figure 4.5). Hold this position for 2 to 3 seconds.
5. Return to the starting position by stepping back when you put the foot down. Repeat with the other leg and gradually make your way across the court to the other doubles sideline.

Figure 4.5

DVD Figure-4 Tuck

Focus: Improve the flexibility of the groin and hips.

Procedure

1. Start at the doubles sideline, facing across the court.
2. Standing on one leg, lift the other leg and, using both hands, cradle the leg. Turn the knee outward while lifting upward on the ankle (figure 4.6). This results in rotation of the hip and a stretch in the deep rotators of the hip. Avoid grabbing for the foot. Instead keep a hand at the ankle to prevent twisting the foot and ankle.
3. At the same time you are cradling one leg, rise up onto the toes of the other, contracting the muscles and coming slightly up off the ground. Release the leg and repeat, alternating between the right and left legs as you proceed across the court.

Figure 4.6

Side Lunge

Focus: Improve the flexibility in the hip and groin.

Procedure

1. Start at the doubles sideline facing the net. Assume an athletic stance.
2. Take a large step sideways into the court, keeping the stationary leg straight (figure 4.7). Bend your stepping leg until you feel a stretch in the groin. Hold this position for 2 to 3 seconds.
3. Resume the athletic stance by bringing the straight leg back under your body. Repeat until you reach the doubles sideline. Reverse direction to work the other leg as you return to the original doubles sideline.

Figure 4.7

Frankenstein Walk

Focus: Improve the flexibility in the hamstrings, gluteals, and lower back.

Procedure

1. Start on the doubles sideline, facing across the court.
2. Hold arms out in front. Swing one leg forward, keeping the knee as straight as possible as you try to touch your toes with the opposite hand (figure 4.8).
3. As soon as you feel a stretch, pull the leg down using your hip and gluteal muscles. Forcefully strike the ground with the front part of your foot.
4. Repeat with the opposite leg, making your way across the court, alternating between the left and right legs.

Figure 4.8

High-Step Trunk Rotation

Focus: Improve the flexibility of the hips and trunk.

Procedure

1. Stand on the doubles sideline facing across the net. Raise the arms to the sides to shoulder level.

2. Begin by bringing the right knee toward the chest while rotating your trunk to the right such that the right knee nearly touches the left elbow.

3. Bring the leg down to the staring position and repeat with the opposite leg while rotating to the left so that the left knee-to-chest pattern nearly brings into contact the left knee and right elbow (figure 4.9).

4. Continue across the court and return to the starting sideline, alternating between right and left legs.

Figure 4.9

Front Lunge

Focus: Improve the flexibility of the gluteals, hamstrings, and quadriceps.

Procedure

1. Stand at the doubles sideline, facing across the court.

2. Take a large step forward with one leg while maintaining an upright posture and looking straight ahead (figure 4.10). Ensure that the knee is properly aligned and moving directly in line with the second toe.

3. Alternate steps with the right and left legs until you have crossed the court one time and returned to the opposite sideline.

Figure 4.10

Torso Rotation

Focus: Improve the flexibility of the trunk, hips, and shoulders.

Procedure

1. Stand anywhere on the court, making sure you have enough room to move freely. Establish a strong base of support.

2. Elevate the arms to shoulder height and gently rotate the arms from one side to the other by twisting the trunk (figure 4.11).

3. Perform twists to both sides, alternating left and right for approximately 30 seconds.

Figure 4.11

Torso Rotation Into Lunge

Focus: Improve the flexibility of the trunk, hips, and shoulders.

Procedure

1. Stand anywhere on the court, making sure you have enough room to move freely. Establish a strong base of support.

2. Elevate the arms to shoulder height and gently rotate the arms from one side to the other by twisting the trunk.

3. As you move from one side to the other, gradually lower the body by bending the knees while pivoting on the balls of the feet (figure 4.12).

4. Perform twists to both sides, alternating right and left for approximately 30 seconds.

Figure 4.12

DVD

Backward Lunge With Trunk Rotation

Focus: Improve the flexibility of the hip flexors.

Procedure

1. Start at the doubles sideline with your back toward the opposite sideline.

2. Take a large step back with the right leg into a lunge position. Gently twist the torso to the left by reaching with the left hand toward the right heel.

3. Return the torso to a good resting posture after reaching while in the squat position. Stand up by driving up on the front leg to the starting position.

4. Step back with the left leg and reach for the left leg while rotating the trunk to the right (figure 4.13).

5. Repeat the sequence until you reach the opposite doubles sideline.

Figure 4.13

DVD Butt Kick

Focus: Improve the flexibility of the quadriceps.

Procedure

1. Stand on the doubles sideline, facing across the court. Place your hands on your buttocks.

2. Begin jogging toward the opposite sideline, exaggerating the knee bend of the heel-to-buttock motion. Try to touch your heels to your hands. Although the heels may not actually touch the hands, the exaggerated bend of the knee increases gradually as you proceed across the court.

3. As you reach the first doubles sideline, turn and return to the starting position, continuing the kicks.

Backward Step Over

DVD

Focus: Improve the flexibility of the groin and hip.

Procedure

1. Start at the doubles sideline with your back toward the opposite sideline.
2. Lift one knee. Rotate the hip so that the knee points out toward the side.
3. Step backward as if you were trying to clear a hurdle as you step (figure 4.14). You should feel the stretch in the groin and hip region.
4. Perform this exercise from doubles sideline to doubles sideline.

Figure 4.14

Arm Hugs

DVD

Focus: Improve the flexibility of the upper back, chest, and shoulders.

Procedure

1. Stand anywhere on the court with the feet shoulder-width apart.
2. Raise the arms to shoulder level and hug yourself, holding this position briefly (figure 4.15a).
3. Then open the arms as wide as possible, trying to "hug the world" (figure 4.15b).
4. Repeat this sequence 10 to 15 times, increasing the stretch and intensity of the exercise as you proceed.

Figure 4.15

Static Stretching

Static stretching still has a place in a tennis player's training program. Certain areas in the tennis player's body become tight from tennis play. Performing static stretching after tennis play and training sessions with particular emphasis on problem areas is still highly recommended (see the sidebar Static Stretching Procedure).

STATIC STRETCHING PROCEDURE

1. Warm up for 3 to 5 minutes if stretching 30 to 60 minutes before exercise. Otherwise perform static stretches immediately after exercise as part of the cool-down.

2. Emphasize slow, smooth movements and coordinated deep breathing. Inhale deeply. Exhale as you stretch to the point just short of pain, then ease back slightly. Hold this static stretch position for 15 to 20 seconds as you breathe normally. Repeat two or three times.

3. You should feel no pain. If it hurts, or if you feel a burning, you are stretching too far.

4. Stretch your tight side first.

5. Stretch only within your limits.

6. Do not lock your joints.

7. Do not bounce.

8. Try to stretch larger muscle groups first, and repeat the same routine each day.

9. If you have areas of extreme tightness, ask a physical therapist or trainer to check your range of motion to gauge your improvement and guide your flexibility training program.

Although the timing of static stretching has changed, the relative importance and effectiveness has not. Stretching the posterior shoulder by performing the Cross-Arm Stretch, in which the athlete pulls the racket arm across the body at chest level, is important for tennis players because of the specific range-of-motion adaptations that occur from repeated high-intensity serving and tennis play. In addition to the Cross-Arm Stretch, players can also perform several repetitions of the Sleeper Stretch. This stretch has gained popularity recently among overhead athletes who lack internal rotation range of motion. Page 62 shows specifically how to perform this stretch in the side-lying, or sleeping, position, which gives the stretch its name.

Additional stretches for the upper body that are important for tennis players include wrist and forearm stretches (pages 62 and 63). Repetitive overuse of the forearm and wrist muscles can lead to tightness from the gripping inherent in tennis play. Performing these stretches before and after tennis play is highly recommended. You may wonder why these stretches can be performed before and after tennis play. Recent research on the shoulder has shown that maximal serve performance is not affected by the use of static stretches immediately before playing. So these static stretches can be used before play, unlike static stretches for other areas of the body.

Recognizing the critical role of flexibility in peak performance and injury prevention, the United States Tennis Association (USTA) Sport Science Committee has put together recommendations for a static stretching program. Flexibility needs are specific to each person and joint. Tests to measure flexibility can identify areas of inflexibility and demonstrate an athlete's progress with a specific flexibility program. (See chapter 3 for specific tests to determine your areas of need.)

In many instances more than one static stretch is included for a body part. Some of these exercises are more basic than others, and some areas of a tennis player's body, such as the shoulder and hip, require greater emphasis. If one area of the body has a particularly limited range of motion, an athlete may want to perform more than one stretching exercise for that area. Once the athlete is able to perform one of the stretches, he or she may progress to a more advanced exercise that places a greater stretch on a particular muscle group. Focus on the areas of the body that are the most inflexible. Stretching only areas that are perceived as the most flexible or easiest to stretch will take time away from stretching areas that need special attention. It also may be counterproductive by decreasing joint stability or promoting imbalances.

STATIC STRETCHES FOR THE SHOULDER AND ARM

Posterior Shoulder Stretch (Cross-Arm Stretch)

DVD

Focus: Improve the flexibility of the shoulder rotators and upper-back (scapular) muscles.

Procedure

1. Stand holding your right arm straight out in front of you. Place your left hand behind your right elbow.
2. Pull across your body with your left hand. Do not allow your trunk to rotate. By placing the outside of your right shoulder and scapula (shoulder blade) against a fence post or door jam, you stabilize the scapula, which greatly enhances the effectiveness of this important stretch.

DVD Sleeper Stretch

Focus: Improve the flexibility of the shoulder rotators and upper-back (scapular) muscles.

Procedure

1. Lie on your dominant shoulder as you would when sleeping on your side.
2. Place your dominant arm directly out in front of you at a 90-degree angle, keeping the elbow bent 90 degrees. You can rest your chin on the front of your shoulder to increase the stabilization of the shoulder during the stretch.
3. Using your opposite arm, push your hand down toward your feet, internally rotating your shoulder (figure 4.16).
4. Hold for 20 to 30 seconds and repeat.

Note: You can make this stretch even more intense by placing your chin against the front of the shoulder you are lying on, pressing it down even more to provide greater stabilization to increase the stretch.

Figure 4.16

Forearm Flexor Stretch

Focus: Improve the flexibility of the flexors and pronators of the forearm muscles.

Procedure

1. You can stand or sit for this stretch. Hold your arm out in front of you with the elbow straight and your palm up.
2. Use the opposite hand to stretch the wrist back (extension), keeping the elbow straight (figure 4.17).

Figure 4.17

Forearm Extensor Stretch

Focus: Improve the flexibility of the forearm extensors and supinators.

Procedure

1. You can stand or sit for this stretch. Hold your arm out in front of you with the elbow straight and your palm down.
2. Use the opposite hand to stretch the wrist down (flexion), keeping the elbow straight (figure 4.18).

Figure 4.18

STATIC STRETCHES FOR THE HIP AND LEG

Hamstring Stretch

Focus: Improve the flexibility of the hamstrings and gluteals.

Procedure

1. Lie on your back. Raise the leg to be stretched to a 90-degree angle at the hip. Support the leg by grasping both hands behind the knee. Keep the opposite leg straight.
2. Straighten the leg and pull it toward the trunk (figure 4.19). Use the hands to gently increase the stretch. Flexing your foot to pull your toes toward your face increases the stretch.

Figure 4.19

Hamstring Superstretch

Focus: Improve the flexibility of the hamstrings and calf muscles.

Procedure

1. Place one leg on a stable surface, such as a table or chair seat.

2. Slowly bend forward at the waist, bringing your trunk toward your thigh (figure 4.20). Flexing your foot to pull your toes toward your face intensifies the stretch.

Figure 4.20

DVD Quadriceps Stretch

Focus: Improve the flexibility of the quadriceps and hip flexors.

Procedure

1. Stand on one leg. Bend the other knee and reach behind you to grasp your foot or ankle (figure 4.21).

2. Keeping the back straight and the buttocks tucked under, pull your heel toward the buttocks and point your knee straight down toward the ground. Do not twist the leg.

Figure 4.21

Seated Groin Stretch

Focus: Improve the flexibility of the groin and inner-thigh muscles.

Procedure

1. Sit with the bottoms of your feet together, knees out, holding on to your toes (figure 4.22).

2. Gently pull forward, bending from the hips to bring the chest toward the feet. Do not round your upper back. Use your elbows to gently push your knees toward the ground.

Figure 4.22

Hip Twist

Focus: Improve the flexibility of the lateral hip muscles and lower back.

Procedure

1. Lie on your back with your knees bent and feet flat on the floor. Place your arms out to the side on the ground to stabilize the upper back or cross your arms across your chest. Place your right ankle outside the left knee.

2. Use the right leg to pull the left leg toward the floor until you feel a stretch along the outside of your hip or lower back (figure 4.23). Keep the upper back and shoulders flat against the floor. The idea is not to touch the floor with the left knee but to stretch within your limits.

Figure 4.23

Piriformis Stretch

Focus: Improve the flexibility of the piriformis muscle.

Procedure

1. Lie on your back with the left knee bent. Place the right ankle just above the left knee.
2. Slowly bring the left knee toward the chest (figure 4.24). You will feel the stretch in the right buttock.

Figure 4.24

Hip Rotator Stretch

Focus: Improve the flexibility of the hip rotators and lateral hip and thigh muscles.

Procedure

1. Lie on your back with your arms out to sides and legs straight.
2. Lift the exercising leg to 90 degrees then allow it to lower across the other leg (figure 4.25). Keep the trunk and both shoulders on the floor throughout the stretch.

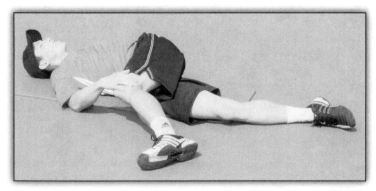

Figure 4.25

Iliotibial Band Stretch

Focus: Improve the flexibility of the iliotibial band.

Procedure

1. Stand with your left hand on a wall, your left leg approximately 3 feet (1 meter) from the wall, and the right leg crossed over the left.

2. Gently push the left hip toward the wall (figure 4.26). Increase the stretch by standing farther from the wall.

Figure 4.26

Calf Stretch

DVD

Focus: Improve the flexibility of the calf muscles (gastrocnemius and soleus).

Procedure

1. Stand with the balls of your feet on the edge of a step. Rest your hand against a wall or fence to help you balance, if necessary.

2. Keeping your right knee straight, lower your right heel until you feel a stretch in the back of your calf (figure 4.27a). Hold this stretch for a few seconds.

3. Slightly bend your right knee and feel an additional stretch in a deeper muscle in the calf (figure 4.27b).

4. Repeat with the left leg.

Note: If a step isn't available or you need a lighter stretch, stand in front of a wall or fence with one leg approximately 2 to 3 feet behind the other, toes pointing straight forward. Keeping the back knee straight and heel on the floor, bend the front knee and lean the trunk forward. Repeat with the back leg slightly bent, heel on the ground, for a deeper stretch.

Figure 4.27

STATIC STRETCHES FOR THE TRUNK

DVD Knees-to-Chest Stretch

Focus: Improve the flexibility of the lower back and gluteals.

Procedure

1. Lie on your back with your knees bent.
2. Bring your knees toward your chest by grasping the lower legs just below the knees (figure 4.28).
3. Hold for 20 to 30 seconds then stretch each leg individually. Pull the right knee to the chest while keeping the left leg straight on the ground.
4. Repeat, pulling the left knee to the chest and keeping the right leg straight.

Figure 4.28

Spinal Twist

Focus: Improve the flexibility of the lower back and hip rotators.

Procedure

1. In a seated position with the left leg extended forward, bend the right knee and place the right ankle outside of the left knee.
2. Bring the left arm around the right knee. Slowly turn the shoulders and trunk to the right looking over the right shoulder (figure 4.29).

Figure 4.29

Additional Methods of Enhancing Flexibility

In addition to static and dynamic flexibility exercises, several other types of flexibility exercises exist. Ballistic stretching involves quick bounces at the motion extremes and has been recommended for some athletic populations. Because it is potentially harmful and offers no significant benefits over other techniques, we do not recommend ballistic stretching for tennis players. Ballistic stretching often elicits the stretch reflex, so that it can actually hinder flexibility by setting off a self-protective mechanism in a muscle, causing it to shorten. Ballistic stretching is potentially injurious because of the danger to exceed the extensibility limits of the tissue being stretched.

Contract–relax stretching is a technique that requires an educated and skilled partner to assist with the stretching process. A brief contraction of the muscle being stretched is initially performed, immediately followed by a static stretch of that muscle or muscle group. The theory is that immediately after the contraction of the muscle, there will be enhanced relaxation of the muscle making the stretching process easier. Physical therapists and trainers often use this technique when working with injured athletes and some research has supported this technique's use. If you are using this technique in your training program, be sure the person helping you has experience with it and is qualified to perform it.

SUMMARY

The information on stretching and warm-up is provided to help tennis players properly prepare their bodies for tennis play and training activities. Players are encouraged to engage in a dynamic warm-up before tennis play and high-intensity workouts and use static stretches after tennis play. Incorporating stretches that target key areas of need and maintaining proper flexibility will prevent injury and enhance performance. The stretching sequences in this chapter are tennis specific and can be used by tennis players at any level.

Chapter 5

Agility and Footwork

To be able to play tennis at a high level, you must develop the ability to move quickly in all directions, change directions often, stop, and start, all while maintaining balance and control to hit the ball effectively. Tennis truly is a sport of continual emergencies because with every shot your opponent hits, the ball can travel at a different velocity with a different type or amount of spin and can land in a different part of the court. Therefore, agility and proper footwork are crucial to good court movement and positioning on the court.

So, although it's important to work on grooving your strokes, don't overlook the importance of working on your movement on the court. Your footwork and movement, just like your tennis strokes, can be improved if you work at it.

SURFACES, EQUIPMENT, AND MOVEMENT

Of all the major sports, tennis is the only one played on a wide variety of court surfaces, even at the highest levels of the game. We estimate that there are almost 1 million tennis courts in more than 200 countries. Court surfaces range from very slow clay courts to very fast grass courts and everything in between. Most rallies last significantly longer on a clay court than they do on a hard or grass court. Research published by the International Tennis Federation a few years ago on both male and female players points out the following percentages of baseline rallies:

French Open (clay)—51 percent of points

Australian Open (Rebound Ace)—46 percent of points

U.S. Open (hard)—35 percent of points

Wimbledon (grass)—19 percent of points

These findings clearly point out the various demands on players and strategies used by players on the four surfaces used at Grand Slam tournaments. Not only are the points longer on certain court surfaces, the patterns of movement change as well. Keep in mind that not every hard court or every clay court plays the same either.

Rackets also have a significant effect on movement skills. With the old wooden rackets, everyone was taught to turn sideways and follow through with the racket toward the target. Modern rackets are made of lightweight materials, allowing players to swing faster and with a different swing pattern. Open stances have become more prevalent, thereby changing the movement patterns players use to get to the ball to hit it and during recovery following contact. For the upper body, this typically means more rotation is involved in the groundstrokes. Players may still step forward toward the ball depending on the situation. However, because of open stances, players generate tremendous force from the inside leg (the leg closest to the ball). This leg also is used in recovery when pushing off to get back to the middle of the court to get in position for the next shot.

POSITIONING

One of the most important things in becoming a good tennis player is to be in the correct position to hit the ball. You must not only have good footwork so you can get to the ball but also have proper balance once you get there. Players need to be in the correct position to provide a solid platform from which to hit the ball.

Balance

Keeping your body and racket under control while you are moving is often referred to as *dynamic balance*. Static balance, or balance without movement, is more easily learned; a typical balanced position is one in which your feet are shoulder-width apart and your center of gravity is directly over your feet. Although this provides a stable base of support, this position is not always possible while playing a point, especially when you are pulled wide for a shot. The key, however, is to try to control your center of gravity as much as possible while you are playing. Proper posture is critical in this regard. Bending at the knees for shots instead of bending at the waist will help you maintain good posture. In addition, keeping your head motionless not only allows you to maintain better balance, but also helps you see the ball better. Keep the head up and face forward to optimize movement efficiency. Reaching or lunging for shots pulls your body off balance, which keeps you from producing powerful shots and slows your recovery.

When responding to an opposing player's shot, your center of gravity cannot be so far outside of your base of support that you are unstable or overcommitted. In tennis, the preparatory movement before such a change of direction is the split step.

Split Step

Although many players are aware of the importance of a split step when preparing for a return of service, it is equally important to focus on the split step in preparation for each of your opponent's other shots. The purpose of the split step is simply to ready the body to move in any direction by putting the leg muscles "on stretch." Typically, the split step involves a slight hop followed by a lowering of the body into the ready position (see figure 5.1). The ready position, with weight on the balls of the feet, knees slightly bent, and feet shoulder-width apart allows a player to initiate the split step instantly. The split step is similar to a skier "unweighting" when making a turn. The unweighting, or hop, is immediately followed by a contraction of the lower leg muscles. The leg muscles are stretched at the landing from the split step and store elastic energy, much like a rubber band does. The energy stored in these muscles allows the player to generate a more powerful and explosive movement to the next ball. The best players actually prepare for their next movement while still in the air by slightly turning the foot closest to the ball in that direction. The foot turn is the result of a whole-leg rotation from the hip. This slight outward rotation at the hip enhances a player's ability for lateral movement.

Figure 5.1   Split step: *(a)* ready position, *(b)* initiation of the split step, *(c)* first step.

First Step

The first step toward the ball is the most important. The split step helps you overcome resting inertia (remember Newton's first law from physics class). Certainly, recognition of where the ball is going and subsequently initiating movement in that direction as quickly as possible helps the player get from point A to point B faster. Tennis along the baseline is often a series of glide steps, with an occasional crossover step when changing directions. However, when absolute speed is needed (for example, when your opponent hits a drop shot), an explosive first step becomes vital to quick movement. You can test your short-distance speed with a 20-Yard Dash test (see chapter 3). First-step explosiveness requires good lower-body power, which also allows a player to accelerate and decelerate quickly.

AGILITY TRAINING

Agility, quite simply, is the ability to change direction efficiently. In a typical match, players need to make more than four directional changes per point, making agility a critical component for being able to move efficiently and get into position to hit the ball. Agility not only requires the muscular strength and power to decelerate and then accelerate in a different direction, but it also depends on flexibility and balance. Great movers typically have great agility and a diverse athletic background that allows them to develop kinesthetic awareness of how the body can move in balance.

The great thing about movement and agility drills is that they often can be integrated into on-court training time and do not necessarily require separate training time. Several tennis-specific drills are included in this chapter.

As you would do with any drill that draws heavily on strength and power, perform these drills when your muscles are fully rested. This means taking appropriate rest between sets and doing these types of exercises at the start of a training session before muscles become fatigued. Quality is more important than quantity.

Maintain peak intensity. If you start to fatigue or you see a drop in intensity, stop the drill or give yourself more rest between efforts. For many people, this may mean performing a drill for only 5 seconds. More advanced players strive to do the exercises outlined in this chapter for 10 to 20 seconds while maintaining technique and explosiveness.

AGILITY DRILLS

Lateral Alley Drill

DVD

Focus: Improve movement, agility, and footwork; improve tennis-specific conditioning when done multiple times or with other agility and movement drills.

Procedure

1. Start outside the doubles sideline facing the net (figure 5.2*a*).
2. Shuffle (side step) into the court, getting both feet over the singles sideline (figure 5.2*b*).
3. Quickly reverse direction and shuffle (side step), getting both feet over the doubles sideline (figure 5.2*c*).
4. Repeat this side-to-side movement pattern for 10 to 20 seconds.

Variation: Perform the drill while holding a racket. Hold the racket in the dominant hand as if you were playing a point.

Figure 5.2

Forward and Backward Alley Drill

Focus: Improve forward and backward movement, agility, and footwork.

Procedure

1. Start outside the doubles sideline, facing into the court (figure 5.3*a*).
2. Run into the court, getting both feet over the singles sideline (figure 5.3*b*).
3. Quickly reverse direction and backpedal, getting both feet over the doubles sideline (figure 5.3*c*).
4. Maintain good body position: head up, upper-body straight, and knees slightly bent. Do not run with your weight on your heels when moving backward.
5. Repeat for 10 to 20 seconds.

Figure 5.3

 ## Lateral Cone Slalom

Focus: Improve lateral movement, agility, and footwork.

Procedure

1. Line up 10 to 12 cones along the baseline about a yard (0.9 meter) apart.
2. Start at one end of the cones, facing the net.

3. Slalom (weave) through the cones using small adjustment steps, moving slightly diagonally forward and backward until you reach the end of the cones (figure 5.4).

4. Facing the net, shuffle (side step) back to the starting position and repeat.

5. Repeat from the other side of the line.

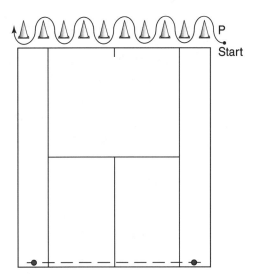

Start

Figure 5.4

Forward and Backward Cone Slalom

Focus: Improve forward and backward movement, agility, and footwork.

Procedure

1. Line up 10 to 12 cones along the baseline about a yard (0.9 meter) apart.

2. Start at one end of the cones, facing the cones (across the width of the court).

3. Weave through the cones using small sideways adjustment steps, moving forward slightly diagonally until you reach the end of the cones.

4. Backpedal through the cones to the starting position and repeat.

Spider Run

Focus: Improve movement, agility, and footwork.

Procedure

1. Start at the center mark on the baseline, facing the net.

2. Turn and sprint right to the corner formed by the baseline and the singles sideline (figure 5.5). Decelerate and touch the corner with your foot.

3. Sprint back to the center mark, maintain control, and touch it with your foot.

4. Sprint to the corner formed by the right singles sideline and the service line. After regaining control, touch the corner and sprint back to the center mark.

5. Next sprint to the T and back to the center mark.

6. Then sprint to the corner formed by the left singles sideline and the service line.

7. Finally, sprint to the corner formed by the left singles sideline and the baseline.

8. Rest for 30 seconds and repeat in the other direction.

Variations

• Pick up a tennis ball at each station and return it to the center mark on the baseline.

• Simulate a shot at each station. Simulate all forehands, all backhands, or a combination, for example, forehand when moving right, backhand when moving left.

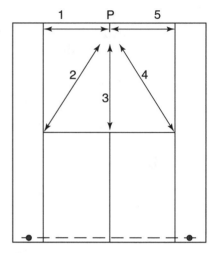

Figure 5.5

DVD Cross Cones

Focus: Improve movement, agility, and footwork.

Procedure

1. Place cones A and B about 5 yards (4.5 meters) apart on the service line so that the center service line (or T) is in the middle of cones A and B (figure 5.6).

2. Place cone C about 4 yards (3.6 meters) from the T on the center service line.

3. Place cone D 6 to 7 yards (5.5 to 6.4 meters) from the T closer to the baseline.

4. Start at the T, facing the net.

5. Shuffle (side step) between cones A and B three to five times then sprint to cone C on a command from the coach.

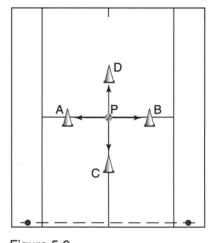

Figure 5.6

6. At cone C, maintain control, turn and sprint to cone D.

7. After decelerating and regaining control, turn and sprint to the T.

8. Resume shuffling between cones A and B.

9. Repeat for 10 to 20 seconds.

Variation: Perform the drill with a racket in your hand. Hold the racket in the dominant hand as if you were playing a point.

Figure 8

Focus: Improve lateral, forward, and backward movement; agility; and footwork.

Procedure

1. Place two cones about 4 1/2 feet (1.4 meters) apart; this is the width of the doubles alley (figure 5.7).
2. Start behind one of the cones, facing the net.
3. Move around the cones laterally and slightly diagonally, tracing a figure 8 around the two cones.
4. The footwork involves small sideways adjustment steps with some small backward and forward adjustment steps.
5. Continue the drill for 10 to 20 seconds.
6. Repeat the drill, starting in front of a cone and facing the net. Move in a forward and backward figure-8 pattern around the cones.

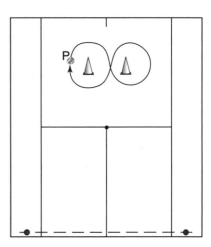

Figure 5.7

Variation: Perform the drill with a racket in your hand. Hold the racket in the dominant hand as if you were playing a point.

Four-Cone Square

Focus: Improve movement, agility, and footwork.

Procedure

1. On a court, place four cones about 6 yards (5.5 meters) apart to create a square (figure 5.8).
2. Starting at cone A and facing the net, sprint to cone B.
3. After regaining control, make small adjustment steps to completely circle cone B.
4. Shuffle from cone B to cone C.
5. After decelerating at cone C, go around C, again making small adjustment steps, and backpedal to cone D.
6. Go around cone D, making adjustment steps, and shuffle (side step) to cone A.

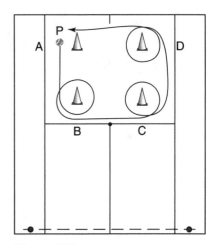

Figure 5.8

7. Repeat, starting at cone D and progressing to C, B, and finally A.

8. Perform this drill two or three times in each direction, resting 20 to 30 seconds between efforts.

Variation: Perform the drill without adjustment steps by sprinting from cone A to B, shuffling to C, backpedaling to D, and shuffling laterally back to A.

 Service-Box Crossover

Focus: Improve lateral movement, agility, and footwork; improve crossover technique, acceleration, and deceleration.

Procedure

1. Start with one foot in the doubles alley and the other foot in the singles court, facing the net (figure 5.9*a*).

2. Using the foot in the doubles alley, cross over in front and move across the court sideways, using crossover steps, until the inside foot gets to the center of the court (figure 5.9*b*).

3. Decelerate and change directions, repeating the crossover movement with the other leg (figure 5.9*c*).

4. Return to the starting position. Continue for 10 to 20 seconds.

5. Repeat two or three times with 15 to 30 seconds of rest between each repetition.

Variation: Cross half the court six times then sprint through the other doubles sideline.

Figure 5.9

Forward and Backward

Focus: Improve forward and backward movement; improve transitions, agility, and footwork.

Procedure

1. Place one cone 5 to 6 feet (1.5 to 1.8 meters) in front of the baseline and a second cone 5 to 6 feet (1.5 to 1.8 meters) behind the court.
2. Start on the baseline, facing the net.
3. In each variation of the drill, move forward and backward, taking a stroke at each cone.
4. Visualize the ball's path over each cone and see yourself hitting a perfect shot.
5. For the forehand/forehand short/deep combination, start on the left side of the cones (if right handed) and alternately stroke a forehand over each cone.
6. For the backhand/backhand short/deep combination, start on the right side of the cones (if right handed) and alternately stroke a backhand over each cone.
7. Perform each drill for 10 to 20 seconds with at least 30 seconds of rest between repetitions.
8. Perform each variation of the exercise two or three times.

Variation: Also perform the drill with the forehand/backhand short/deep combination and the backhand/forehand short/deep combination. During these combinations, you must use a little more dynamic balance and agility because you must cross between the cones and turn your body to perform the strokes properly.

Court Widths or 17s

Focus: Improve movement, agility, footwork, acceleration, and deceleration.

Procedure

1. Start at the doubles sideline, facing across the court.
2. Accelerate and run across the court to the opposite doubles sideline.
3. Reaching the opposite doubles sideline counts as one court width, or one repetition.
4. After decelerating and regaining control, accelerate back to the starting sideline, completing the second repetition.
5. Repeat until you complete 17 court widths.
6. Record your time. A good time for boys is less than 50 seconds, for girls less than 55 seconds, and for 12U less than 60 seconds. You can also use this drill as a fitness test.

Note: This is a great conditioning tool used by many basketball teams.

Horizontal Repeater

Focus: Improve movement, agility, and footwork.

Procedure

1. Start at the doubles sideline, facing the net.
2. Shuffle (side step) to the center service line (figure 5.10).
3. Sprint back to the starting position.
4. Turn and sprint across the court to the opposite doubles sideline.
5. Shuffle back to the center line.
6. Sprint back to the doubles sideline.
7. Turn and sprint back through the starting position. You should start and finish at the same spot.
8. Perform two or three repetitions with 30 seconds of rest between each repetition.

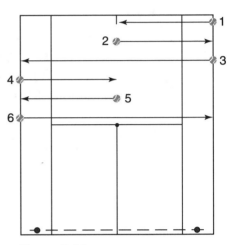

Figure 5.10

Hollow-Half Horizontal Repeater Variation: After performing steps 1 through 4, instead of immediately performing steps 5 through 8, stop and walk back to the starting position and repeat the sequence.

Variation: Perform the drill with a racket in your hand. Hold the racket in the dominant hand as if you were playing a point.

Vertical Repeater

Focus: Improve forward and backward movement, agility, footwork, acceleration, and deceleration.

Procedure

1. Start at the baseline, facing the net.
2. Sprint to the net (figure 5.11).
3. Backpedal to the service line.
4. Sprint to the net again.
5. Turn and sprint back to the baseline.
6. Perform this exercise two or three times with 30 seconds of rest between repetitions.

Variation: Perform the drill with a racket in your hand. Hold the racket in the dominant hand as if you were playing a point.

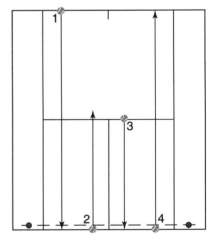

Figure 5.11

Diagonal Repeater

DVD

Focus: Improve all-around movement, agility, and footwork.

Procedure

1. Start at a corner formed by the baseline and a singles sideline, facing the net.

2. Shuffle (side step) along the baseline to the center mark on the baseline (figure 5.12).

3. Shuffle (side step) back along the baseline to the starting corner.

4. Sprint diagonally to the net where it meets the opposite singles sideline.

5. Backpedal along the singles sideline to the baseline.

6–9. Repeat these movements from this back corner.

10. Perform two or three repetitions with 30 seconds of rest between repetitions.

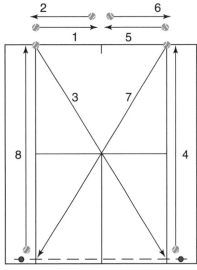

Figure 5.12

Hollow-Half Diagonal Repeater Variation:
Instead of performing steps 5 through 10, stop and walk back to the starting position and prepare to immediately start the next repetition.

Variation: Perform the drill with a racket in your hand. Hold the racket in the dominant hand as if you were playing a point.

Volley Drill

DVD

Focus: Improve movement, agility, footwork, and volley technique.

Procedure

1. Place two cones, equidistant from the center service line, about 6 inches (15 centimeters) in front of the service line. They should be 8 to 10 feet (2.4 to 3 meters) apart from each other.

2. Start the drill just above the service line toward the baseline, facing the net.

3. Alternately move in front of each of the cones and perform a volley stroke (figure 5.13).

4. Recover to the starting position after each volley and perform a split step.

5. Visualize hitting the perfect volley each time with perfect footwork.

Figure 5.13

6. Do this drill for 10 to 20 seconds or for a set number of shots. Perform the drill two or three times with 30 seconds of rest between repetitions.

Variations

- Perform a low volley in front of each cone. Be sure to get down well with the legs instead of bending forward at the waist.
- React to a hand signal from your coach whether to hit a forehand or backhand volley or a forehand or backhand low volley.

 ## Forehand and Backhand Agility

Focus: Improve movement, agility, and footwork.

Procedure

1. Start at the center mark on the baseline, facing the net.
2. Turn and sprint to the forehand side and perform a stroke even with the singles sideline. Visualize hitting the shot and use proper technique.
3. Recover with a crossover step and a shuffle, or side step, back toward the center mark.
4. From the center mark, turn and sprint to the backhand side to perform a stroke even with the singles sideline.
5. Again recover with a crossover step and a shuffle, or side step, back toward the center mark.
6. Repeat this movement pattern for 10 to 20 seconds or for a specified number of strokes. Perform the entire drill two or three times with 30 seconds of rest between repetitions.

Variations

- For an added challenge, try the next drill, Condensed Deuce Court.
- React to a hand signal from the coach whether to hit a forehand or backhand.

 ## Condensed Deuce Court

This drill is similar to the Forehand and Backhand Agility drill, but it requires quicker footwork because you move only between the sideline and the center mark.

Focus: Improve movement, agility, and footwork.

Procedure

1. Start the drill along the baseline at the middle of the deuce court (for a right-handed player) or the middle of the ad court (for a left-handed player).

2. Turn and sprint to the forehand side and perform a wide forehand.

3. Recover with a crossover step and a shuffle, or side step, back toward the center mark.

4. After recovering back toward the center of the deuce court, turn and perform a backhand stroke at the center mark.

5. Again recover with a crossover step and a shuffle, or side step, back toward the starting position.

6. Repeat this movement pattern for 10 to 20 seconds or for a specified number of strokes. Perform the entire drill two or three times with 30 seconds of rest between repetitions.

Variation: Perform the drill on the ad side (for a right-handed player) or the deuce side (left-handed player), hitting only forehands. Visualize hitting inside out or inside in from the wide backhand side.

Mini Tennis Z-Ball

DVD

Focus: Improve movement, agility, footwork, and reaction time.

Procedure

1. This game is played with two or more players. Players use only the service boxes.

2. Play and score the game like a tiebreaker. Instead of a racket and tennis ball, use a Z-ball (reaction ball). Catch and toss the ball underhand (figure 5.14).

3. Using underhand throws, play tennis with your partner by tossing the Z-ball into your opponent's service box.

4. The ball must bounce once in the service box before it is caught. The ball must be caught before it bounces a second time.

Figure 5.14

5. Play until one player wins a tie-break game to 7.

Note: If more than two players are involved, play the game using table tennis rules. Players alternate in one at a time.

Variation: To make the drill easier, instead of a Z-ball use a tennis ball.

Medicine Ball Tennis

Focus: Improve movement, agility, footwork, core strength, and leg strength.

Procedure

1. This game is played by two or more players. Use only the service boxes. Play and score the game like a tiebreaker.

2. Instead of a racket and tennis ball, use a medicine ball. Catch the ball and toss it from the same side of the body, mimicking a forehand or backhand groundstroke.

3. Be sure to load your outside leg (the leg closest to the ball) behind the ball when you catch it to store energy in the muscles. This will allow you to use the entire kinetic chain to generate force when tossing the ball back.

4. Let the ball bounce once in the service box before catching it.

5. Play until one player wins a tie-break game to 7.

Note: If more than two players are involved, play the game with table tennis rules. Players alternate in one at a time.

SUMMARY

When you watch the top players in the world, you'll notice that the best players are often the best movers as well. Proper footwork and agility are critical to success on the court. If you can't get to the ball, it doesn't matter how good your strokes are. In addition, tennis is much more than just running in a straight line. Changing direction frequently is a huge part of the game. Players need to learn to go from shuffle steps to sprints to backpedaling in a matter of a few seconds. The drills in this chapter give you ways to improve your agility. You'll be amazed at your progress if you perform these drills regularly.

Chapter 6

Speed and Quickness

As mentioned in chapter 5, agility and footwork are vital to success in tennis. In addition, being able to sprint for a drop shot or from one side of the court to the other can be equally beneficial to your tennis success. A tennis coach many years ago told us that bad players run slow and swing fast, while good players run fast and swing slow. Although it can be argued that good players nowadays both move fast and swing fast, there is a nugget of truth in this statement.

So, although it's important to work on grooving your strokes, don't overlook the importance of working on your movement on the court. Your footwork and movement, just like your tennis strokes, can be improved if you work at it.

IMPORTANCE OF SPEED WHEN MOVING

Speed is the time it takes to get from point A to point B, and it is an important attribute in tennis. Speed development depends on muscular strength and power. Training that develops these attributes will help improve on-court movement and performance. Tennis players can use exercises such as plyometrics to improve speed. There are several key things to note about plyometrics.

Plyometric exercises place a great deal of stress on muscles and joints. Start with low-level plyometric exercises such as jumping rope or alley drills before progressing to more advanced drills such as box jumps. Establish a suitable strength base before you begin plyometric exercises. In fact, the National Strength and Conditioning Association recommends players be able to squat two times their body weight before engaging in high-level, high-intensity plyometric leg exercises. A good resource on plyometrics for tennis, which presents exercises and progressions, is *Jumping Into Plyometrics* by Don Chu.

Although adolescent players can use low-level plyometrics, more advanced exercises should be integrated into a training program only after puberty. Senior players, especially those with lower-limb injuries, should also take care when engaging in plyometrics because of the stress they place on the body.

Interestingly, although speed is deemed important in tennis, players rarely attain top running speed during match play. In approximately 80 percent of points, the player does not move more than 30 feet (9 meters) from the position where he or she started. Yet within those 30 feet (9 meters), a player can only attain 75 percent of his or her peak running speed. So although we will present drills to improve running speed, two even more important concepts are quickness and acceleration.

QUICKNESS

In tennis a quick first step gives a player a distinct advantage. Being able to instantly recognize and react to the shot the opposing player is using can be the difference between getting to a ball or not, attacking a ball, and hitting a winner as opposed to pushing back a defensive shot. Quickness has been described as the ability to read, react, and explode: *read* and process cues as to what is happening, *react* with the appropriate response, and *explode* with quickness and power to maximize the time you have to set up for your shot.

All of these factors can be grouped into what is called response time, the time it takes for a player faced with a decision or cue to make the appropriate movement. Response time takes into account both the time it takes to process the information and choose a response and the time it takes for the muscles to contract and the movement to occur. Accordingly, total response time depends on a player's reaction time (which deals with anticipation and the speed at which information is processed by the brain) and movement time (which concerns how quickly the muscles are activated and the movement executed).

> Response time = reaction time + movement time

By performing tennis-specific movement and agility drills, players can improve both reaction time and movement time, resulting in improvements in on-court movement. These improvements are exhibited by better agility and quickness.

REACTION TIME

Much of quickness depends on anticipation. A player who is able to predict what is going to happen has an advantage over an opponent. Even if the player is not able to predict exactly what is going to happen, if he or she can at least narrow the options to a manageable number, the player has gained an advantage.

The first key to developing good anticipation skills is developing the ability to read cues from the opposing player. Where do you look when you watch your opponent? Recent research has shown that one of the differences between expert and novice players is where they focus their attention as their opponent hits the ball. Novice players' eyes drift around without focusing on any one particular area. Expert players focus on the racket and lower part of the dominant arm. Focusing on this area allows them to anticipate the type of shot and direction the ball will be hit. It has even been shown that expert players can predict where the body is going to go when other parts of the body are blocked from view, eliminating cues that could be detected from that part of the body. The key is to focus on the upper body and the swing path of the racket as much as possible.

Second, know the possible shots that can be hit based on the court geometry and your opponent's position. A player drawn out wide and hitting on the run is likely to hit down the line rather than come across court. Eliminating possibilities will also allow you to react more quickly to a shot. The more choices you have, the longer it takes you to choose the right response. For example, a player who knows he or she is only going to have to move left or right (two choices) is going to be able to react more quickly than a player who has to choose between moving forward, backward, left, or right (four choices). By knowing the possibilities available to the opponent, you can improve your court position and take control of the point.

Third, know the tendencies of your opponent. Some basic scouting can help you anticipate the shots your opponent will use in specific situations. Maybe your opponent likes to serve down the T at 40-all. Knowing this can give you an advantage when facing this situation.

Finally, develop well-rehearsed motor patterns. If you have ever tried to learn a new skill, you know that if you want to do it correctly you often have to slow the movement. However, with practice, the movement becomes faster and faster until the response is automatic. That is how you want your movements and responses to be in tennis, and that is why you need to develop your movement skills while using proper technique.

Players can use many drills to improve movement efficiency, but drills also provide an opportunity to train cue identification and anticipation. For example, when performing a drill, it is important to initiate the drill using a tennis-specific cue or action. When performing a movement drill in which the player needs to move to the right or left, rather than shout "Right" or "Left," the coach holds a tennis ball out to one side or the other to indicate which way the player should go. In this way the player reacts to the ball and focuses on the appropriate part of the body to pick up cues.

ACCELERATION AND DECELERATION

Acceleration is the ability to increase speed rapidly, in other words, how well a player can go from a dead stop to full speed. Research shows that the greatest acceleration occurs in the first 8 to 10 strides a player takes and that technique and mechanics play a critical role in determining how fast a player can accelerate. This is good news! Many players think speed and acceleration are genetically determined, and they are to some extent. Still everyone, regardless of genetics, can improve acceleration by learning some basic running-form drills that teach proper running technique. These drills are outlined later in the chapter.

Deceleration is the ability to slow rapidly. Although a player can attain up to 75 percent of his or her top sprinting speed within 30 feet (9 meters), many people expect to decelerate the body from a dead run to a complete stop in one or two strides. This can place a great amount of stress on the muscles and structures that support the knees, hips, and ankles because muscles contract eccentrically to absorb large amounts of energy. Many strength coaches believe that the ability to decelerate safely and efficiently should be developed before players work on acceleration.

Exercises that develop strength and explosive power such as plyometrics and Olympic lifts are essential for laying the groundwork for acceleration and deceleration. Focus on training the body for deceleration first, then acceleration. Also, work to perform explosive exercises on one leg at a time. There are not many instances in tennis when both feet are on the ground at the same time. Players need to be able to maintain balance while generating force when only one foot is on the ground.

Figures 6.1, 6.2, and 6.3 show a simple lower-body plyometric progression that emphasizes deceleration, acceleration, and then single-leg power with cue recognition.

Jump from a midsized plyometric box and absorb the force of the landing. Land in an athletic position with proper posture. The athletic position is similar to the ready position described in chapter 5: weight on the balls of your feet, knees slightly bent, and feet shoulder-width apart.

Jump down from a midsized plyometric box and jump straight up.

Jump down from a midsized plyometric box and explode into a run to the right or left depending on a cue from the coach. The coach can use a tennis balls to cue the player.

Figure 6.1   Phase 1: Deceleration

Figure 6.2 Phase 2: Deceleration followed by acceleration

Figure 6.3 Phase 3: Deceleration followed by acceleration with reaction to a cue

RUNNING MECHANICS AND FORM

Basic running-form drills are described in this section. Follow these pointers to enhance running technique.

Keep the head in line with the body. Don't lift the chin up or tuck it down toward the chest. You should be able to draw a straight line from the ankle through the knee, hip, shoulder, and ear as the support leg pushes off the ground.

Take advantage of gravity. Gravity is your friend. In most normal instances you want the body to be in balance with the center of mass directly over the base of support. However, when accelerating or decelerating, moving the center of mass outside the base of support and deliberately throwing the body out of balance can help get the body moving. When done appropriately, gravity will pull the body in the direction you want to move.

Use the legs appropriately. When raising the knee, dorsiflex the ankle (pull the toes toward the shin) and land on the balls of the feet. Drive the feet into the ground with the foot making contact just under or slightly behind the body's center of mass.

Minimize foot contact time. Quick feet lead to quick movements. Hit the ground and move. The feet should feel like they are popping off the ground.

Use the arms. The arms contribute significantly to running efficiency. Pump the arms in synch with the legs to get more speed. Use a racket to make drills as tennis-specific as possible.

Work on various court surfaces if you can. Movement on hard courts is dramatically different than movement on clay. Practice on various surfaces to get the feel for what it takes to accelerate, decelerate, and change direction while maintaining your balance.

It is important to understand ground reaction forces when talking about running mechanics. Remember Newton's third law—for every action there is an equal and opposite reaction. When the foot hits the ground, the ground pushes back. Many players tend to overstride, or reach with the foot, in an attempt to get more speed. However, when the foot is in front of the body, the reaction force is directed back toward the body, causing the player to slow down.

RUNNING-FORM DRILLS

DVD High-Knee March, No Arms

Focus: Improve running and movement technique.

Procedure

1. Stand on the doubles sideline, with the body relaxed and little or no weight on your heels. Relax your upper body and do not use your arms.

2. Lift your left knee high while bringing your heel toward your butt (figure 6.4).

3. Keep your toes up. Imagine you are pulling your toes toward your shin. Do not twist at the hips or shoulders.

4. Drive the leg back down toward the ground, taking a small step forward.

5. Repeat with the other leg. Continue this movement as you march across the court twice.

Note: Keeping the knee up, heel up, and toe up decreases the distance from the hip to the foot, allowing for faster turnover, or stride frequency.

Figure 6.4

High-Knee March, With Arms

DVD

Focus: Improve running and movement technique.

Procedure

1. This drill is done like the High-Knee March, No Arms but adds the arm swing.
2. When the arm is next to your side, the elbow should be bent at a right angle.
3. Swing the right arm forward as you bring the left knee up and vice versa for the left arm and right knee (figure 6.5).
4. Raise the hand to about shoulder or mouth level. As the arm swings forward from the shoulder, the angle of the arm may decrease slightly.
5. As the arm swings back, the hand should pass the hip. As the arm continues back, the angle of the arm may increase slightly. This movement, in which the elbow goes back and up and the hand passes the hip serves as your accelerator and is often called "throwing down the hammer."
6. Continue this movement pattern as you march across the court two times.

Figure 6.5

Note: The arms are important during sprinting. Many tennis players run with their arms out wide, twisting their bodies, or without using their arms at all.

Skip

DVD

Focus: Improve running and movement technique.

Procedure

1. Stand at the doubles sideline, looking into the court.
2. With your arms at your sides, bend your elbows to 90 degrees.
3. Swing the right arm forward as you bring the left knee up and vice versa for the left arm and right knee, much like the motion made in High-Knee March, With Arms.
4. Perform a skip or slight hop with each step forward as you raise the opposite knee. Lean forward slightly as you skip.
5. Bring the foot down so that it contacts the ground under the body.
6. Continue the movement pattern across the court two times.

Skip With Leg Extension

Focus: Improve running and movement technique.

Procedure

1. Stand at the doubles sideline, looking into the court.
2. Lift one knee as performed in High-Knee March, No Arms.
3. As you lift the knee, perform a skip, or slight bounce, off the ground (figure 6.6).
4. When the knee reaches its highest point, extend the foreleg forward.
5. Just after extending the leg, paw the ground with the foot so that the ball of the foot hits the ground directly under the body.
6. Keep the upper body relaxed and do not use the arms.
7. Repeat with the other leg while slowly moving forward. Continue across the court two times.

Figure 6.6

Note: Think "knee up, foreleg reach, paw the ground" as you do this drill.

 ## Butt Kick

Focus: Improve running and movement technique.

Procedure

1. Stand at the doubles sideline and rise onto the balls of your feet.
2. Place your hands on your butt, palms facing out.
3. Alternately raise the heels to the buttocks, trying to kick your hands, while running slowly forward.
4. Keep the upper body relaxed and do not use your arms.
5. Stay off the heels. Do not twist at the hips or shoulders. Keep the knees pointed down.
6. Perform this drill across the width of the court two times, from doubles sideline to doubles sideline.

High-Knee Run, No Arms

Focus: Improve running and movement technique.

Procedure

1. Stand at the doubles sideline and rise onto the balls of your feet.

2. Alternate lifting the left and right knee up high while slowly moving forward (figure 6.7).

3. Put the foot down under the body. To avoid braking or putting the foot down too far forward, remember to "keep your nose over your toes."

4. Lean forward slightly. Do not twist at the hips or shoulders or use the arms. Keep the upper body relaxed.

5. Perform the drill across the width of the court two times, from doubles sideline to doubles sideline.

Note: This drill differs from High-Knee March, No Arms in that the motion is closer to running than just marching and is similar to a football player running through the tires.

Figure 6.7

High-Knee Run, With Arms

Focus: Improve running and movement technique.

Procedure

1. This drill is performed like High-Knee Run, No Arms but uses the arms.

2. When the arm is next to your side, the elbow should be bent at a right angle.

3. Swing the right arm forward as you bring the left knee up and vice versa for the left arm and right knee (figure 6.8).

4. Raise the hand to about shoulder or mouth level. The angle of the arm may decrease slightly.

5. As the arm swings back, the hand should pass the hip. The angle of the arm may increase slightly. This movement serves as your accelerator and is often called "throwing down the hammer."

6. Continue with this movement pattern as you run across the court two times.

Figure 6.8

Note: This drill differs from High-Knee March, With Arms in that the motion is closer to running than just marching and is similar to a football player running through the tires.

Variation: Pump the arms as quickly as possible. The legs move as fast as the arms pump. The faster the arms pump, the faster the legs move.

SUMMARY

Performing these drills regularly will help you improve your speed and quickness, allowing you to get to the ball early. This in turn will help you get set up quickly for each shot, which will allow you to use proper technique with good balance. Remember, you can't hit the ball if you can't get to it.

Chapter 7

Core Stability Training

One of the most important areas of concentration for training athletes in the last few years has been the core. Training for tennis is no exception, and core training forms an important part of the resistance training program for tennis players at all levels.

In a broad sense, the core can be thought of as the central third of the human body. More descriptively, the core encompasses the spine, hips, pelvis, thighs, and abdomen. The actual core musculature consists of the abdominals (rectus abdominis, transversus abdominis, and the internal and external obliques), lower back (muscles such as the erector spinae, latissimus dorsi, and multifidus), and some of the muscles of the pelvis and hips such as the gluteals, quadratus lumborum, and hip flexors. The key functions of these muscles are to maintain the stability of the region and, perhaps most important for sport, to transfer the energy generated by the lower body to the upper body.

For the legs and arms to move and function properly, there must be proper stability in the core. This has led to the term *core stability,* which can be thought of as the ability of the core musculature to control the position and movement of the trunk over the lower limbs. The end result of proper core stability is the optimum production and transfer of force and motion to the upper body to enhance human performance.

When most people think of the core, they immediately think of abdominal muscles. Although the abdominal muscles are a major part of the core, they are just one part of the musculature that comprises this important area. The main or central abdominal muscle is called the rectus abdominis, which runs from the rib cage to the pelvis (see figure 7.1).

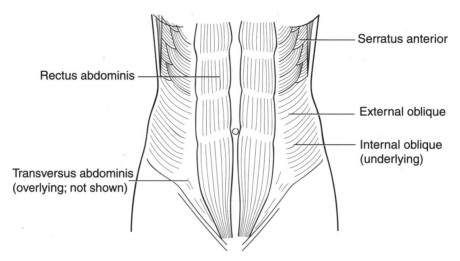

Figure 7.1 Abdominal muscles.

Reprinted, by permission, from S. Cole and T. Seaborne, 2003, *Athletic Abs* (Champaign, IL: Human Kinetics), 7.

However, in addition to the rectus abdominis, several other stabilizers of the trunk comprise the abdominal complex, including the transversus abdominis (TA), as well as the muscles on the sides, commonly referred to as "love handles," the internal and external obliques. The oblique muscles are mainly responsible for rotating the body, which is important for tennis players. These muscles in the front and sides of the core are complemented in the lower back by several important muscles that complete the cylindrical core of muscles that stabilize the trunk. Core back muscles include the erector spinae, latissimus dorsi, and gluteals. Other muscles play a role in core stability and include a group of small muscles on the floor of the pelvis and the groups of muscles that move and stabilize the hip joints.

UNDERSTANDING HOW THE CORE FUNCTIONS

To best demonstrate the ways in which the muscles of the core are used during tennis, let's review the pertinent mechanics and muscles used during the tennis service motion (see figure 7.2).

During the service motion, the abdominal muscles eccentrically contract, or lengthen, to stabilize the spine as it extends back, allowing the upper body to position the hand and arm in the required cocked position. The back extensors concentrically contract, or shorten, during this movement, while the internal and external oblique muscles assist with the rotation of the torso. Additionally, the abdominals and back extensors on the right side of the body are shortening to bend the trunk to the side, while the same muscle pairing on the left side of the body is lengthening, allowing this motion to occur with control. As you can see, a complex interplay exists between concentric and eccentric muscle activity among the core muscles to enable just one part of the service motion to occur. This complex interaction is required for the thousands of serves a player performs while training or competing in a tennis tournament. Tennis players need core strength, power, and muscular endurance.

Several studies provide the rationale for the emphasis on core stabilization training for tennis players. Years ago, abdominal muscle function in tennis players was monitored during the performance of actual tennis strokes, including groundstrokes, serves, and volleys. This research showed that on virtually all tennis shots, the abdominals contracted intensely (near their maximum capability) to stabilize the trunk. This study showed how much tennis players actually need and rely on these important muscles during tennis performance.

Figure 7.2 Sam Querrey demonstrates the cocking position of the tennis service motion.

A second study measured the strength of the abdominal and lower-back muscles using sophisticated machinery called an isokinetic dynamometer. High-level junior tennis players were asked to flex and extend their spines using their abdominal and lower-back muscles while the machine measured the force they could produce.

This study showed significant abdominal muscle strength in these elite tennis players, but weak lower-back muscles compared to the normal population. This highlighted the importance for sports medicine and fitness professionals to not just strengthen the abdominals like they had done for years using Sit-Up exercises, but also to focus on the lower-back muscles and think of the trunk as a cylinder to be trained all the way around from the front to the back.

Finally, a third study was done to determine whether tennis players have greater strength during side-to-side rotation in

CONDITIONING TIP

Elite-level tennis players show greater abdominal strength compared to their lower-back strength. Specific exercises are required to balance the trunk muscles to prevent injury and enhance performance.

CONDITIONING TIP

Research shows that elite-level tennis players have similar strength when rotating to either side. Be sure to include training exercises that encourage balanced strength in rotating to both the left and right in your training program.

one direction than in another (i.e., a muscle imbalance). Because it is estimated that up to 75 percent of all strokes in the modern game of tennis involve forehands and serves (which, for a right-handed player, requires forceful trunk rotation to the left), it was questioned whether elite-level tennis players had equal strength when rotating to the forehand and backhand sides. Players rotated in an isokinetic dynamometer, simulating both forehand and backhand groundstrokes.

Results showed that players rotate with equal strength to both the forehand and backhand sides. Therefore, training the core in tennis players must involve rotational training to both the forehand and backhand sides.

TRAINING THE CORE

Now that we have discussed what the core and core stability are and some of the characteristic demands tennis play places on the core, we will present some of the critical components that make up a training program for this important group of muscles. The following are key concepts:

- Use methods and exercises that strengthen the entire abdominal complex.
- Use movement patterns that include trunk rotation whenever possible.
- Include multiple sets of exercises to encourage muscular endurance.
- Think of the core as being a cylinder. Include the muscles in the front, back, and sides.
- Ensure that rotation in both directions is used to promote balanced strength.

Throughout this book we have emphasized the importance of testing and identifying where each player's needs are (chapter 3). Core training is no different. Using the two core stability tests presented in chapter 3 (Sit-Up on page 24 and Core Stability on page 25) can help not only to identify the need for training but also to gauge progress as retesting occurs following training.

To gain muscular endurance in the core, build up to multiple sets of 15 to 20 repetitions of each exercise. The co-contraction exercises are more time based, so build up to multiple sets of 30 seconds.

ABDOMINAL EXERCISES

Drawing In

Focus: Improve the strength of the transversus abdominis and the stabilizing core muscles.

One of the first strategies that can be applied when performing exercises to develop the core involves the drawing-in maneuver. This maneuver can be applied when doing a simple exercise like an Abdominal Curl or during a complex exercise like a Lunge With Rotation. Performing the drawing-in technique has been shown to increase the intensity of muscle involvement in the transversus abdominis and other stabilizing core muscles to increase the effectiveness of any core exercise.

Procedure

1. Lie on your back on a stable surface or exercise ball or stand upright.
2. Draw in, or suck in, your abdomen (figure 7.3). This is similar to the action you would do if trying to get into a pair of pants that are just a little too tight.
3. Another way to think of this is to pull the belly button back toward the spine.

An excellent example of two core exercises for the abdominal muscles during which the drawing-in maneuver can be simultaneously performed are the traditional Abdominal Curl on Exercise Ball and the Dead Bug.

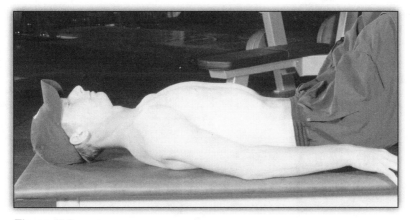

Figure 7.3

Abdominal Curl on Exercise Ball

Focus: Improve the strength of the trunk muscles and improve balance.

Use of an exercise ball for nearly any exercise increases the activity of the trunk muscles by forcing you to stabilize and balance during the exercise movement. The Abdominal Curl exercise uses only a small range of motion because flexing the spine more than 45 degrees serves mainly to strengthen the hip flexor muscles and therefore detracts from the primary goal of the exercise—strengthening the abdominals.

Procedure

1. Lie with your back on an exercise ball with your feet flat on the floor and hands across your chest.

2. Using your abdominal muscles, lift your shoulders and upper body (figure 7.4a). Remember to draw in your abdominal muscles. Do not lift your torso past 45 degrees.

3. Lower the shoulders and upper body to the starting position.

Advanced variations

• Use a medicine ball and partner to provide overload and explosiveness during the exercise (figure 7.4b).

• Couple the upward (flexing) motion of the trunk with rotation to engage the oblique muscles.

Figure 7.4

Dead Bug

Focus: Improve the strength of the trunk muscles and spinal stabilizers.

The practicality of the dead-bug exercise is that it activates the trunk muscles and stabilizes the spine while the arms and legs are moving, similar to what tennis players have to do while moving on the court and during the execution of virtually any tennis motion.

Procedure

1. Lie on your back with your hips and knees bent 90 degrees and arms flexed to 90 degrees and pointing straight up in the air (figure 7.5a).

2. Draw in your abdominal muscles (see drawing-in technique). While keeping your back stable, alternately lower your right leg and left arm, keeping your other arm and leg stationary (figure 7.5b).

Figure 7.5

3. As you lower your left arm and right leg, focus on keeping your back and torso braced, working the abdominal and lower-back muscles. Hold this position for about 1 second and return to the starting position.

4. Lower the left leg and right arm while keeping the other arm and leg stationary. Continue this sequence, alternating arm and leg pairs, until you fatigue and cannot maintain the stable trunk position.

Note: If this exercise is too difficult and you find yourself unable to stabilize your trunk as you lower the arm and leg, try lowering only one leg, keeping the arms stationary. Once this becomes easy, progress to using the alternating arm and leg pairs.

TRUNK ROTATION EXERCISES

In addition to traditional abdominal exercises, important exercises for tennis players involve trunk rotation.

Seated Ball Rotation

Focus: Improve trunk rotation, working all the core muscles.

This exercise uses an exercise ball to challenge the stability of the player and engage multiple muscle groups and uses a medicine ball to create overload and develop explosiveness. This exercise simulates the stroke patterns of forehands and backhands and can be varied by changing the weight of the ball, direction of the tosses (down the line or crosscourt) as well as the distance between the partner tossing and the exercising player.

Procedure

1. Sit on an exercise ball with your feet on the ground approximately shoulder-width apart.
2. Holding a 4- to 6-pound (1.8- to 2.7-kilogram) medicine ball, simulate a forehand groundstroke, throwing the medicine ball to a partner who is 5 to 10 feet (1.5 to 3 meters) away (figure 7.6). The partner can be sitting on an exercise ball or standing on the ground.
3. Repeat multiple times (e.g., sets of 30 seconds) in crosscourt and down-the-line patterns.
4. Perform similar patterns using the backhand groundstroke pattern.

Figure 7.6

Russian Twist

Focus: Improve trunk rotation, stabilization, and balance.

The Russian Twist is another core stabilization exercise that involves tennis-specific rotation while requiring high levels of muscular stabilization to maintain posture and balance. The exercise ball compromises the stability of the player, while the weight of the medicine ball complements the rotational movement inherent in this exercise. One important component of this exercise is the maintenance of the hip and knee position throughout the exercise, which is accomplished by the core stabilizers.

Procedure

1. Lie faceup with an exercise ball under your shoulder blades. Your feet should be shoulder-width apart on the floor and your knees bent 90 degrees. Ensure that your hips are in neutral extension (don't let your butt sag!). With your shoulders flexed 90 degrees and hands pointing upward, hold a medicine ball or weight (figure 7.7a).

2. From this position, keeping the abdominal muscles drawn in and buttocks squeezed together, rotate alternately to the left and right slowly and with control (figure 7.7b). Keep the pelvis and torso aligned properly. This exercise also challenges your overall balance as you rotate from side to side.

Figure 7.7

Lunge With Rotation

Focus: Improve the strength of the core stabilizers and quadriceps.

Procedure

1. Stand and hold a weight or medicine ball at shoulder level with the arms extended outward and elbows straight.

2. Take alternating steps forward into a lunge position. Bend the front knee no more than 90 degrees and make sure your knee stays pointed directly over your second toe and does not extend past your toes. When you reach the descent phase of the lunge, rotate the upper body and trunk to the left, pause a second, return to the center, pause a second, and then turn to the right, pausing a second.

3. Return the ball to the forward position and lunge forward with the other leg. Repeat this exercise for several sets of 15 to 20 repetitions. Maintain proper posture during the lunge. Avoid bending forward at the waist and keep the eyes looking forward.

CO-CONTRACTION EXERCISES

Although not truly rotational exercises, two additional exercises are appropriate for this section because they involve muscular co-contraction of many of the core muscles. Co-contraction refers to the simultaneous activation of multiple muscles or groups of muscles during an exercise or activity. Exercises that promote this type of muscular work are often preferred for improving the stability of a joint or series of joints in the human body. TV Watching and the Side Plange are two excellent exercises for improving core stability.

TV Watching

Focus: Improve core stability.

TV Watching involves maintaining a properly aligned trunk and hip position during several sets that last a predetermined time. Also important is maintaining proper neck and upper-back alignment. Several sets of 30 seconds in this position are an excellent initial goal, increasing the time as your strength and ability improve.

Procedure

1. Assume a position on both elbows and the toes (figure 7.8). It is important to maintain straight alignment; don't let your bottom sag or stick up in the air.

Figure 7.8

2. Keep the neck in neutral alignment. Look straight down toward the floor at a point slightly in front of you. Maintain this position for several sets of 30 seconds.

Side Plange

DVD

Focus: Improve the strength of the obliques, quadratus lumborum, and gluteus medius.

The Side Plange is particularly important for the obliques and muscles on the side of the body, such as the quadratus lumborum and gluteus medius. Proper alignment is imperative for this exercise, and we recommend multiple sets on both sides. Several sets can serve as an initial goal. Because research shows that balancing the development of trunk muscles is important for maintaining a tennis player's health, exercise both sides of the body.

Procedure

1. Lie on your side and position yourself on your elbow and the outside of the bottom foot (figure 7.9*a*). Maintain straight body alignment, looking straight ahead.

2. Hold this position for several sets of 30 seconds.

Variation: Secure a piece of elastic tubing several feet in front of you. With your non-weight-bearing hand, perform several sets of 15 repetitions of a rowing exercise while remaining stabilized in the plange position (figure 7.9*b*).

Figure 7.9

LOWER-BACK EXERCISES

It is important for tennis players to work on the muscles of the lower back to properly balance the muscles of the core.

Superman

Focus: Improve the strength of the lower-back muscles.

This is the simplest exercise to perform for the lower-back muscles (also called the erector spinae, or extensor muscles).

Procedure

1. Lie on the ground with a pillow under your pelvis, if needed.
2. Simultaneously lift your feet and hands off the ground to achieve the "flying" position (figure 7.10a).
3. Hold for 1 to 2 seconds before slowly returning to the start position.
4. During the exercise, draw in the abdominal muscles and tense the gluteals (squeeze the muscles of the buttocks together) to further challenge the core musculature.

Variation: Alternate raising only the left arm and right leg together, then the right arm and left leg (figure 7.10b).

Figure 7.10

Arm and Leg Extension

Focus: Improve the strength of the lower-back muscles.

Procedure

1. Assume an all-fours (quadruped) position on your hands and knees.
2. Draw in your abdominals and contract your gluteals.
3. Extend your left arm and right leg. Hold for 1 or 2 seconds, trying to maintain proper balance. Return to the starting position.
4. Extend your right arm and left leg (figure 7.11). Hold for 1 or 2 seconds then return to the starting position.

Advanced variations

- Use hand weights to provide greater resistance.
- Lie on an exercise ball.

Figure 7.11

Cobra

Focus: Improve the strength of the lower-back muscles.

This is another fine exercise that uses trunk extension and also activates muscles in the scapular (shoulder blade) region. Perform multiple sets of this exercise, making sure to engage the gluteal muscles and squeeze the shoulder blades together at the top of the extension.

Procedure

1. Lie facedown on an exercise ball, with your abdomen contacting the ball.
2. Hold a dumbbell in each hand. With elbows bent at 90 degrees, lower your forearms toward the floor (figure 7.12*a*).

3. Extend your trunk and hips upward (like a cobra raising its head), rolling slightly forward on the ball (figure 7.12*b*).

4. Hold that position for 1 to 2 seconds and return to the starting position.

Variation: Move the arms to an overhead position, which is more difficult.

Figure 7.12

ADVANCED CORE EXERCISES

For the advanced phase of core training, several exercises ultimately challenge the player's ability to cocontract muscles, maintain proper posture, and perform controlled movements over an exercise ball. Knees to Chest, Knees to Chest With Rotation, and the Diagonal Leg Tuck all require high levels of core stabilization and body control to ultimately train the core musculature.

Knees to Chest

Focus: Improve posture and muscle control through co-contraction.

Procedure

1. Place your hands shoulder-width apart on the ground with an exercise ball supporting your legs just between your knees and ankles. You are supporting yourself on your arms and the ball.

2. While maintaining proper alignment with the abdominals drawn in and the gluteals engaged, bring both knees toward your chest.

3. After a brief pause, extend your knees slowly, returning to the starting position.

Knees to Chest With Rotation

Focus: Improve posture, muscle control, and rotation through co-contraction.

Procedure

1. Place your hands shoulder-width apart on the ground with an exercise ball supporting your legs just between your knees and ankles. You are supporting yourself on your arms and the ball.

2. While maintaining proper alignment with the abdominals drawn in and the gluteals engaged, rotate your trunk and hips and bring both knees along a diagonal path toward your chest (figure 7.13).

Figure 7.13

3. After a brief pause, extend your knees slowly, returning to the starting position.

4. Repeat, rotating to the other side.

Note: Adding rotation to the Knees to Chest exercise increases the difficulty and the tennis application.

Diagonal Leg Tuck

Focus: Improve posture, muscle control, and rotation through co-contraction.

Procedure

1. With an exercise ball under your legs between the knees and ankles, place both hands on the ground approximately shoulder-width apart. You are supporting yourself on your arms and the ball.

2. Take your left leg from the ball and move it diagonally across the front of your body, reaching the left knee toward the right hip (figure 7.14).

3. Hold the end position, and then slowly return to the starting position.

4. Repeat, taking the right leg and moving it diagonally toward the left hip.

Figure 7.14

SUMMARY

Many types of exercises can improve core stability. The exercises in this chapter address the inherent demands placed on the trunk during tennis play. Implementing these exercises in a complete conditioning program will help improve core stability, decrease injury risk, and enhance performance. These exercises are an important part of an overall strength and conditioning program for tennis players. They can be skillfully integrated into an overall strength and power training program, discussed in chapter 8.

Strength and Power Training

Players such as Andy Roddick and James Blake have the ability to hit the ball just as hard in the first game of a match as in the final game of the fifth set. These professional players have committed themselves to performing strength and power exercises that allow their muscles to function at the highest level. This chapter defines common terms and outlines critical components of a strength training program and provides examples of tennis-specific exercises to improve muscular strength and endurance.

Strength training is a type of exercise that requires the muscles to move or attempt to move against some type of opposing force. *Strength* is the maximum amount of force a muscle can produce. Tennis players must have high levels of muscular strength and, because of the repetitive nature of the game, must also be able to repeatedly contract their muscles. The ability to repeatedly contract a muscle or group of muscles is referred to as muscular *endurance*. *Power* is the amount of work done per unit of time and can be thought of as the explosiveness of a muscle or muscle group. Muscular power is a function of strength times speed. Training your muscles for tennis must address all three areas: strength, power, and endurance.

TYPES OF RESISTANCE TRAINING

Several types of resistance are used in developing muscular strength. *Isometric,* or static, strength training refers to a type of training that uses isometric muscle contractions. An isometric contraction of the muscle is one in which no shortening or lengthening of the muscle fiber takes place. No joint movement occurs with this type of training. An example of an isometric exercise is placing the palms of your hands together in front of your chest and pushing them against each other. This isometric exercise elicits a contraction of the pectoral and biceps muscles among others. Contraction times of 6 seconds are usually applied with isometrics to get the most benefit from this type of strength training. Isometrics are not typically used for tennis training because of their lack of joint movement. Because tennis is a rapid, dynamic sport that requires powerful, repeated contractions of the muscles during body movement, more dynamic forms of strength training are recommended.

Isotonic resistance is characterized by a constant weight or tension and is a more dynamic form of strength training that can be used to train tennis players. In this form of strength training, actual shortening and lengthening of the muscle fibers occurs, along with joint movement. An example of an isotonic exercise is a Biceps Curl with a 5-pound (2.3-kilogram) weight in which the elbow joint moves. The muscle fibers shorten (concentric contraction) as the hand and weight move toward the shoulder, then lengthen (eccentric contraction) as the hand and weight are lowered. This shortening and lengthening of the muscle fibers during training is important because tennis requires these types of muscle contractions in every stroke and body movement. Typically, eccentric contractions are used to decelerate and control or stabilize the body, and concentric contractions produce movement and accelerate the body. Isotonic exercises can be performed with body weight; free weights, such as dumbbells, medicine balls, elastic tubing or bands; and many types of weight machines.

There is no single best form of isotonic exercise for a tennis player. Each form has advantages and disadvantages. For example, an advantage of using body weight is that it always is available; you carry it with you wherever

James Blake trains hard so that he can reach as many balls at the end of a match as he does in the first set.

you go. However, you cannot easily change your body weight to provide greater resistance as you get stronger.

Free weights are cost effective but require greater control during lifting because they don't offer a guided path or movement track like isotonic resistance machines do. The use of free weights forces you to stabilize the weight in all directions while moving the weight in the primary movement pattern. This works the secondary muscle groups that stabilize the exercising joints, but it also requires greater skill and supervision to compensate for having less control.

One additional benefit of isotonic resistance machines is the ability of the machine to vary the resistance during the range of motion used during exercise. Look at the pulley system on many resistance machines. Instead of being perfectly round, many are kidney shaped. This unique shape of the cam or pulley on the machine changes the resistance during the exercise, usually making the weight heavier in the middle of the motion and lighter at the beginning and end of the motion, where the body's musculoskeletal system is least efficient.

Another type of isotonic resistance uses elastic tubing or elastic cords. This form of resistance is desirable because it is cost effective, easy to carry on trips, and effective because the farther you stretch the cord, the greater the resistance you generate.

Whatever type of isotonic exercise you do, the important factor is movement. The joints move and the muscles lengthen and shorten to mimic the types of actions you perform when hitting serves, groundstrokes, and volleys. Most of the exercises in this chapter and throughout this book are isotonic exercises and use free weights, elastic tubing or bands, and weight machines.

Isokinetic resistance uses a constant velocity and changing amounts of resistance. It requires the use of a highly technical and expensive machine, which makes it impractical for most players to include in their training. Isokinetic machines are used extensively in injury rehabilitation and in research and have given sport scientists important information about the strengths and weaknesses of the musculoskeletal system of tennis players.

SINGLE-JOINT AND MULTIPLE-JOINT FORMS OF STRENGTH TRAINING

Within each type of resistance used to increase strength are two primary forms of exercise. These two forms are single-joint or multiple-joint exercises. In a single-joint exercise, one primary joint and muscle group are worked. For example, the Leg Extension exercise involves only movement at the knee joint and works primarily the quadriceps muscle. The Squat is an example of a multijoint exercise that works the gluteals, quadriceps, hamstrings, calf muscles, and others, with movement occurring at the hip, knee, and ankle. Both types of exercises are beneficial to tennis players, but multijoint exercises work more muscles and joints simultaneously and certainly are more time efficient. Multijoint exercises, such as the Squat and Lunge, require balance, proper form, and training, but they are considered to be more functional.

Single-joint exercises are especially beneficial when it is necessary to strengthen a particular muscle group to alleviate a muscle imbalance. An example of this will be covered extensively in chapter 11, Solid Shoulder Stability, and involves a tennis player's dominant shoulder. Repetitive tennis training leads to preferential development of the muscles in the front of the body (internal rotators of the shoulder) because of the use of those muscles during the acceleration phases of the serve and forehand. This creates a muscular imbalance in the shoulder as the external rotators, which are extremely important for stabilizing the shoulder and decelerating the arm, become underdeveloped and overshadowed by the powerful internal rotators. Tennis players use special exercises involving mainly single-joint exercises to help balance shoulder strength in the dominant arm and to prevent injury and enhance performance.

ADAPTATIONS TO STRENGTH TRAINING

Adaptations to resistance training can be broken into two primary forms: neural and morphological. *Neural adaptations* involve the nervous system and its response to resistance training. Neural adaptations can occur in as little as two weeks following the initiation of a resistance training program. When you feel stronger after a week or two of lifting weights, this is primarily due to the nervous system becoming more efficient in the way it recruits, or talks to, the muscle. This in turn makes you feel stronger, even though little change has occurred within the muscle structure itself.

Morphological, or structural, adaptations involve the actual structure of the muscle. Some debate still exists among scientists regarding the exact mechanism of this muscular adaptation. One theory, hypertrophy, explains the increase in the overall size of the muscle as an increase in the cross-sectional area of the existing muscle fibers in the muscle—the muscle fibers that you have get bigger. The second theory, hyperplasia, states that the increase in overall size in the muscle in response to training occurs when the existing muscle fibers split, resulting in a greater number of muscle fibers. Regardless of the mechanism of muscular adaptation, scientists agree that it takes at least 6 weeks for this type of improvement to occur with training. Therefore, when starting a strength training program for tennis, realize that although you may experience immediate improvements in the way you feel, it will take at least 6 weeks for true changes to occur in the muscle itself.

Changes in body composition are associated with strength training programs over a 6- to 24-week duration. Studies show an increase in the percentage of lean body mass (muscle, bone, and so on), resulting in a lower overall percentage of body fat.

Misconceptions regarding strength training are prevalent among the athletic and general populations. One of the most common myths among tennis players is that lifting weights will make players bulky and muscle bound and have a negative effect on speed and tennis strokes. This misconception is most easily addressed by educating players and having them follow a strength training program specifically for tennis players. A tennis-specific strength training program does not involve heavy, maximal-effort lifts, but instead uses light to moderate resistance in a relatively high-repetition format that builds strength and muscle endurance, not solely bulk and size.

Another myth associated with resistance training is that it will cause stiffness and loss of flexibility. Again, a resistance training program specifically geared for tennis players used along with a comprehensive flexibility program (outlined in chapter 4) will prevent a loss of flexibility, optimize performance, and prevent injury.

DESIGNING A TENNIS-SPECIFIC STRENGTH TRAINING PROGRAM

Developing a needs analysis is the first step in designing a strength training program for any athlete. Figure 8.1 outlines some of the elements used to determine an athlete's needs based on the demands of the sport.

NEEDS ANALYSIS

Exercise movements
- Muscles used
- Joint angles
- Contraction type (eccentric or concentric)

Energy system (metabolism) used
- Estimated contribution from aerobic and anaerobic metabolism
- Work:rest cycles, performance duration, frequency

Injury prevention
- Most common sites (shoulder, trunk, elbow, knee)
- Player's history of injury

Figure 8.1   Athletic needs and demands for tennis.

Adapted by permission from S.J. Fleck and W.J. Kraemer, 2004, *Designing Resistance Training Programs*, 3rd ed. (Champaign, IL: Human Kinetics), 154.

The concept of specificity is of vital importance. Every resistance exercise program must contain exercises that address the demands inherent in the sport or activity the athlete performs. Knowledge of the biomechanical demands of the sport is also important in the design of a program. Roetert and Ellenbecker performed a study to determine the velocity of the racket head during the first and second tennis serves in elite junior players. Contrary to what is often believed, biomechanical analysis showed that the racket moves about the same speed during both the first and second serves, meaning the muscles must work just as hard during both serves to produce and maintain the racket head speed.

Biomechanical analysis also helps sport scientists to design strength programs for tennis players. One example is with shoulder exercises. Analyzing the tennis serve, scientists have shown that the shoulder is raised only to about a 90-degree angle with the body at ball contact. The reason the racket is so high over a player's head during a serve is that the trunk is bent at an angle that allows the shoulder to remain about 90 degrees and still let the player hit the serve with maximum efficiency. Awareness of this biomechanical information leads us to recommend exercises for the shoulder that do not raise the arms higher than they are during actual tennis play, in this case above shoulder level. The following sections provide guidelines for developing a tennis-specific strength training program.

Sets

A set is a group of repetitions. Typically, 2 to 6 sets of an exercise are required to improve strength and muscular endurance. For tennis, usually 2 to 4 sets of an exercise are recommended. Research performed on high-level collegiate tennis players compared the effectiveness of a 9-month strength training program in which one group trained using only 1 set of each exercise throughout the training period. This was compared to a second group of players who trained using a varied (periodized) program that used multiple sets of each exercise throughout the training program. Results of this important study clearly showed superior improvements in strength, tennis performance, and body composition in the group of players who trained using a multiple-set training program. This study coupled with the knowledge of the highly repetitive nature of tennis play and the high volume of training and practice required for player development have led to the recommendation that tennis players use multiple sets of resistance training exercises.

Repetitions

The number of repetitions performed per set not only determines the amount of work done but also regulates the amount of weight lifted and therefore the intensity of the exercise. Sets of 3 to 6 repetitions are normally used to develop power and strength because the higher resistance loads bring about fatigue during the small number of repetitions. Athletes performing sets with more repetitions use less weight than they would when performing sets of 3 to 6 repetitions. Sets of 10 to 15 repetitions develop muscular strength and local muscle endurance. Sets with 20 to 25 repetitions are mainly used for low-intensity muscle endurance and are geared more for endurance athletes. High-repetition sets with very light weights are often used during the early phases of injury rehabilitation.

What is the optimal number of repetitions in a set for a tennis player? Most experts recommend sets of 10 to 15 repetitions because they provide a strength training and muscular-endurance stimulus, both of which are required for tennis. The higher number of repetitions also means the athlete will use a lighter weight.

Intensity

Set the intensity of an exercise (determining how much weight to use) by using the repetition maximum, or RM, system. In this system athletes select an appropriate weight for a set of exercises that will allow them to perform the desired number of repetitions without breaking proper form and will cause them to feel significant fatigue within the muscle during the last 1 or 2 repetitions of the set. For example, for most players, a 2-pound (0.9-kilogram) weight for 10 repetitions of a Biceps Curl would probably not provide enough resistance to cause fatigue by the 9th or 10th repetition. Likewise a weight of 50 pounds (23 kilograms) would be far too heavy for 10 repetitions of a Biceps Curl unless you were a 250-pound (113-kilogram) American football player. Properly applying the repetition maximum system takes some trial and error when beginning a strength training program.

Rest

One factor closely tied to the specificity of a resistive exercise is rest. In tennis, the average point lasts 10 to 15 seconds followed by 20 seconds of rest. Therefore, the program for a tennis player should emphasize 20-second rest periods between sets. This work-to-rest cycle provides a stress to the muscles similar to the one used in actual tennis play and metabolically stresses the systems used to provide energy to the working muscles just like when you're playing tennis. Additionally, to optimize time during workouts, because the time needed to perform a complete conditioning program for tennis is precious and limited for all players, perform a lower-body exercise, such as the Lunge, after working a muscle group in the upper body, for example the biceps. This allows the biceps to recover without taking long periods of inactivity between exercises.

Frequency

Typically, strength training programs include rest between exercise sessions. Depending on what other elements a player is emphasizing in his or her total conditioning program and where in the periodized training program the player is (see chapter 10 for a complete discussion of periodization), the frequency of strength training can range from once per week to three or four times per week. Most general strength training programs recommend three times per week to build strength, with a day of rest between training sessions. Some players may lift weights every day but alternate the muscle groups and body areas they work so that the working muscles get a day of recovery.

Movement Cadence

The speed at which the weight is moved has a tremendous effect on the quality of the workout. Everyone has seen people working at the gym with too much weight, moving the weight rapidly from start to finish just to complete their repetitions. Emphasize a slow, controlled movement when working with weight machines, free weights, or elastic tubing or bands. A slower, more controlled movement ensures that you raise and lower or push and pull the weight, working the muscle in both the shortening (concentric) and lengthening (eccentric) phases, just like you do during tennis play.

In this chapter and throughout this book, we present and recommend exercises that complement traditional resistance exercises, which use slow, controlled movements and body weight, bands, tubing, free weights, and weight machines. These complementary exercises are called plyometrics and consist of more explosive and rapid movements in a special sequence. Plyometric exercises are characterized by an initial lengthening, or eccentric contraction, immediately followed by an explosive concentric contraction. For the lower body, body weight is typically used as the primary resistance during plyometric exercises; for the upper body, medicine balls and occasionally elastic tubing or bands are used. Research has consistently shown the effectiveness of plyometric exercises for athletes, including tennis players.

Table 8.1 shows which muscles are used during tennis strokes. Target these frequently used muscles with a tennis-specific strength training program that emphasizes both concentric and eccentric actions.

TENNIS-SPECIFIC RESISTIVE PROGRAM

This chapter provides the general information and background for resistive exercise training and key, tennis-specific exercises that use multiple forms of resistance that fit into nearly any player's training situation regardless of the availability of weight machines or sophisticated

Table 8.1 Muscles Used in Tennis Drives, Volleys, and Serves

Forehand drive and volley	
Action	**Muscles used**
Push off	Soleus, gastrocnemius, quadriceps, gluteals
Trunk rotation	Obliques, spinal erectors
Forehand swing	Anterior deltoid, pectorals, shoulder internal rotators, elbow flexors (biceps), serratus anterior
One-handed backhand drive and volley	
Action	**Muscles used**
Push off	Soleus, gastrocnemius, quadriceps, gluteals
Trunk rotation	Obliques, spinal erectors
Backhand swing	Rhomboids and middle trapezius, posterior deltoid, middle deltoid, shoulder external rotators, triceps, serratus anterior
Two-handed backhand drive	
Action	**Muscles used**
Push off	Soleus, gastrocnemius, quadriceps, gluteals
Trunk rotation	Obliques, spinal erectors
Backhand swing, nondominant side	Pectorals, anterior deltoid, shoulder interior rotators
Backhand swing, dominant side	Rhomboids and middle trapezius, posterior deltoid, middle deltoid, shoulder external rotators, triceps, serratus anterior
Serve and overhead	
Action	**Muscles used**
Trunk rotation	Obliques, spinal erectors
Knee and hip extension before impact	Quadriceps, gluteals
Arm swing	Pectorals, shoulder interior rotators, latissimus dorsi, triceps
Arm extension	Triceps
Wrist flexion	Wrist flexors

Reprinted by permission from USTA, 1993, *Strength Training for Tennis*, (White Plains, NY: USTA Player Development Publication Department), 18-19.

machinery and equipment. Review chapter 7 for a complete discussion of core training as well as chapter 11 for detailed information on training the shoulder. In this chapter, we also present specific training programs that can be performed while traveling and present concepts important for integrating a training program during competition or between tournaments.

ADDITIONAL FACTORS

1. **Don't lift weights right before you play tennis.** You don't want to be fatigued while you attempt to perform skill-oriented motor tasks such as serves, groundstrokes, and volleys. It is better to perform resistive exercise sessions on days when tennis workouts are lighter and you can lift weights after you have completed the skill-oriented aspects of your on-court tennis workout.

2. **Every good program must be updated and changed based on the principle of overload.** If you always use a 2-pound (0.9-kilogram) weight to do 10 repetitions of the Biceps Curl, in time the exercise will become very easy. To avoid training at too low an intensity level, add resistance when you no longer fatigue by the end of the set. Some athletes increase the number of reps by 3 to 5 with the same weight, then when that becomes easy, they return to the original number of repetitions per set but use a slightly heavier weight. This progression is an important part of a complete conditioning program for tennis.

3. **Avoid compensation.** If you use too much weight, you will use bigger muscle groups and improper movement patterns that could produce injury. Stay within your own limits of resistance, not the level of your friends or opponents! We recommend some degree of supervision or feedback during your resistance exercise program. Have a qualified strength and conditioning specialist, physical therapist, athletic trainer, or coach monitor or at least periodically check your strength and conditioning exercises. Performing a resistance training exercise improperly is far worse than not performing the exercise at all.

LOWER-BODY EXERCISES

Research conducted on elite tennis players shows that lower-body strength is the same on both the left and right sides. Therefore, lower-body training for tennis players should focus on both legs to ensure balanced strength unless one leg has been injured or is underdeveloped structurally. That being said, for exercises in which both legs perform the exercise movement simultaneously, such as the Leg Press, also train each leg independently to isolate each leg and ensure an optimal training stimulus.

Leg Press

Focus: Improve the strength of the quadriceps, hip extensors, and calves.

Procedure

1. Several types of leg press machines are available, but nearly all use either a seated or supine (lying on your back) position. Position yourself in the device so that your hips and knees are bent approximately 90 degrees (figure 8.2a).

2. From the starting position, perform the basic leg press motion of extending the hips and knees simultaneously until the knees reach nearly full extension (figure 8.2*b*).

3. Slowly return to the starting position.

Variations

- To increase the number of exercising muscles during this exercise, place a medicine ball between your knees and squeeze it throughout the exercise to keep it in place.

- Decrease the weight and perform multiple sets of the Leg Press using each leg independently.

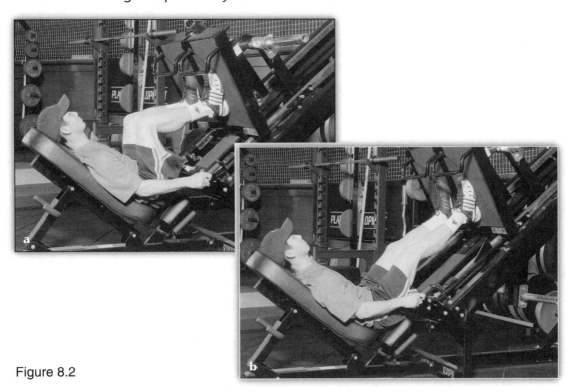

Figure 8.2

Plyometric Leg Press

Focus: Improve the strength of the quadriceps, hip extensors, and calves.

Procedure

1. Begin in the starting position for the Leg Press.

2. Imagine that the plate where you place your feet is divided by a cross into four zones. Begin with both feet in the top left zone and push off the platform in an explosive manner that causes your feet to come off the platform slightly.

3. Land into the top right zone, absorbing the landing. Immediately push off in the same fashion, landing in the bottom right zone.

4. Repeat the sequence, landing in the bottom left zone.

5. Perform 10 to 15 revolutions through all four zones until your legs become fatigued. In addition to the workout for your legs, you will feel your abdominals working as you suspend your legs and hold them against gravity between zones.

Leg Extension

Focus: Improve the strength of the quadriceps.

Procedure

1. This exercise is typically performed on a knee extension machine.

2. In a seated position, adjust the machine so that the resistance bar rests on your shin about 2 inches (5 centimeters) above the ankle.

3. From a bent position, straighten the knees just short of fully straight and return to the starting position.

Note: If you have had knee problems, use only portions of the range of motion to minimize the stress to your kneecap as it glides against the end of your femur. See the variations for more information.

Variations

- Perform the exercise starting with the knee bent 90 degrees and extend the knee only 45 degrees (low arc).

- Perform the exercise starting from the nearly straightened position and bend the knee 30 to 40 degrees (high arc). This exercise is used in rehabilitation following knee injury and minimizes the compression in the knee during the exercise.

- Work each leg independently to ensure that both legs are balanced.

Alternative equipment: Use elastic tubing or bands instead of a knee extension machine by securing one end of the band under a table leg and the other around your leg near the ankle.

Partial Squat

Focus: Improve the strength of the quadriceps and hips.

Procedure

1. Begin by standing with the feet shoulder-width apart, looking straight ahead. You can hold a dumbbell in each hand or hold a medicine ball in both hands behind your head and neck to provide resistance. Or you can loop a piece of elastic tubing or an athletic band under both feet and wrap it in each hand or bring it up over the back of the

shoulders to provide resistance as you progress through the Partial Squat.

2. Bend the knees and flex the hips to descend slowly, keeping an upright posture (figure 8.3*a*). Avoid bending forward at the waist. As your knees bend, make sure they do not buckle inward and that each knee is aligned over the second toe of each foot.

Figure 8.3

3. Bend to 60 to 90 degrees of knee flexion in a controlled fashion, then pause at the low position for 1 to 2 seconds before returning to the start position.

Note: If you have difficulty with your posture in this exercise, stand with your back against a wall and an exercise ball placed in the small of your back. Perform the Partial Squat exercise leaning against the ball as you descend and ascend.

Variations

- Perform the Partial Squat on one leg to further challenge your balance system, which is important for optimal tennis performance.
- Stand on a foam platform or mat during the exercise to further challenge your balance (figure 8.3*b*). Be sure to look forward and not at the ground as you perform the exercise.

Plyometric Step-Over

DVD

Focus: Improve the strength of the lower body.

Procedure

1. Hold a medicine ball behind your head and neck. Stand to the side of a step platform.
2. Place your inside leg on the platform (figure 8.4*a*). Your outside leg remains on the ground. Push off the outside leg across the platform so that the inside leg lands on the other side of the step platform on

the ground and the push-off leg lands on top of the platform (figure 8.4b).

3. Repeat going side to side in an explosive manner for sets of 20 to 30 seconds. As you are able, reach farther and farther with the outside leg to increase the range of motion of the exercise. Perform multiple sets, resting 20 seconds

Figure 8.4

between each set. Be sure to look forward once you are comfortable with the exercise to ensure that you maintain an upright posture.

DVD **Low-to-High Chop**

Focus: Improve the strength of the lower body and trunk.

Procedure

1. Secure a piece of elastic tubing to a fence or net post just above ankle level. Stand with your feet approximately shoulder-width apart in an athletic stance. Grasp the band with both hands near the outside of your knee (figure 8.5a).

2. Starting from a position of knee and hip flexion, explosively straighten the knees and hips while thrusting upward in a diagonal motion across your body (figure 8.5b). Your trunk will rotate slightly.

Figure 8.5

3. While you are exploding upward with your legs and torso, raise your arms in an upward chopping motion in a diagonal pattern as well. Hold the end point for only a second and return to the starting position.

4. Perform the same number of repetitions by performing the diagonal pattern to the other side.

Lunge

DVD

Focus: Improve the strength of the lower body.

Procedure

1. Stand with your feet shoulder-width apart. Start by performing the lunge using only your body weight. For greater resistance, grasp a dumbbell in each hand or hold a medicine ball behind your head and neck with both hands.

2. Keeping an upright posture, step forward with one foot, absorbing the load of the body and bending the front knee into a lunge position (figure 8.6). To protect your knee, allow the front knee to bend no more than 90 degrees. Ensure that your knee is directly aligned over the second toe of the foot.

3. Immediately push off the front foot to return to the starting position.

4. Complete multiple sets, alternating right and left leg lunges.

Figure 8.6

Variations

• Lunge to the side and 45-degree angle positions, including a 45-degree cross step for more tennis specificity to closely mimic on-court movement patterns.

• Have a partner stand behind you, looping a long piece of elastic tubing or band around your waist. The partner provides resistance as you step forward into your lunge. This not only provides resistance but also challenges your balance.

Calf Raise

Focus: Improve the strength of the gastrocnemius and soleus.

Procedure

1. From a standing position, come up onto your toes, raising your heels off the ground (figure 8.7). For added resistance, hold a dumbbell in your hand.

2. Hold for 1 to 2 seconds and slowly return to the start position.

Variations

- Place a wood block under the toes to force the ankle to move against a larger range of motion during the exercise.

- To work the deeper calf muscle, the soleus, sit in a chair with your knees bent 90 degrees. Place a barbell or dumbbell across your thighs to produce resistance. Raise your heels off the ground, hold for 1 to 2 seconds, and return to the starting position. Place a block of wood under the toes to make this exercise more challenging.

Figure 8.7

Multihip

Focus: Improve the strength of the core and lower extremities.

Procedure: Many types of multidirectional hip machines exist. The main advantage of this machine-based exercise is that you can easily work the hip in all four directions of movement (in, out, forward, and backward) with minimal setup or change. Some machines require you to perform the exercise from a seated position; others require a standing position. If you perform the standing version, both legs work at the same time—the stance limb (for stabilization) and the moving leg.

Monster Walk

DVD

Focus: Improve the strength of the hip and core.

Procedure

1. Stand with your feet slightly less than shoulder-width apart in an athletic stance. Loop an elastic band around your ankles. (Note: The band should not be so heavy that it limits your ability to move and take steps. A light band will go a long way in providing resistance as you exercise, and you can always progress to a heavier band if you feel the band is too easy.)

2. Take a lateral step with one leg while keeping tension on the band (figure 8.8).

3. Bring the other leg toward the leg you initially stepped with, planting the foot while there is still tension in the band. Repeat the step.

Variation: Perform this exercise on court by taking side steps from one doubles sideline to the other, working both hips. You can also take steps forward

Figure 8.8

and diagonally; however, the side-to-side movements are helpful for the hips and core. Keep the head up and maintain an upright posture rather than staring at the ground during this exercise.

Elastic Band Kick

Focus: Improve the strength of the hip and core.

Procedure

1. Stand with your legs about shoulder-width apart, your weight on one leg, and a band looped around both ankles, similar to the starting position of the Monster Walk exercise.

2. Keeping an upright stance and slight bend in the knee of the supporting leg, quickly move the other leg to the side approximately 12 inches (30 centimeters and back to the starting position), keeping light tension in the band, for 30 seconds.

3. Rest and repeat the exercise, making rapid forward kicking motions approximately 12 inches (30 centimeters).

Figure 8.9

4. After another rest period, make rapid kicking motions in a backward direction approximately 12 inches (30 centimeters) for another 30 seconds.

5. Repeat this series to fatigue on the same leg. Then switch to the other leg. You will notice that both the standing leg and working leg work hard and that this exercise challenges your balance. It requires great skill to successfully execute the kick in all three directions while maintaining proper balance.

Variation: Use a foam balance pad or platform to further challenge your balance system (figure 8.9 on previous page). If you are traveling and do not have a balance platform, you can stand on a pillow.

Hamstring Curl

Focus: Improve the strength of the hamstrings.

Procedure

1. Sit on a chair or bench with your knee bent 90 degrees. Loop a piece of tubing or elastic band around your ankle and secure the other end to a sturdy object such as a post.

2. After securing the tubing, position yourself far enough away from the attachment point of the tubing to create slight tension in the band when your leg is extended straight in front of you (figure 8.10*a*).

3. Slowly and in a controlled manner, bend your knee 90 degrees (figure 8.10*b*).

4. Return the leg to the starting position.

Note: Be sure to maintain controlled movement during this exercise. A common error is to let the leg rapidly snap back to the starting position rather than using your muscles to decelerate the motion.

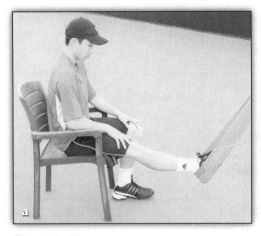 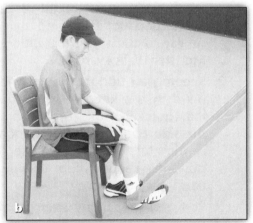

Figure 8.10

TRUNK EXERCISES

Review chapter 7, Core Stability Training, for a complete discussion of the specific demands tennis places on the core and for specific exercises to train this part of the body. The exercises listed here can be performed using weight machines; however, the preferred method of core training uses body weight, exercise and medicine balls, and other resistance mediums to foster greater muscular activation and challenge.

In addition to the exercises in this chapter, the exercises described in chapter 7 should be used as part of a comprehensive core strength program:

Drawing In (page 101)

Abdominal Curl on Exercise Ball (page 102)

Dead Bug (page 103)

Seated Ball Rotation (page 104)

Russian Twist (page 105)

Lunge With Rotation (page 106)

TV Watching (page 106)

Side Plange (page 107)

Superman (page 108)

Arm and Leg Extension (page 109)

Cobra (page 109)

Knees to Chest (page 111)

Knees to Chest With Rotation (page 111)

Diagonal Leg Tuck (page 112)

Back Extension

Focus: Improve the strength of the spinal extensors and gluteals through a machine exercise.

Procedure

1. Sit in the machine leaning forward 90 degrees or slightly more. The resistance pad should rest across your shoulder blades.

2. With your arms crossed across your chest, eyes looking straight ahead, and your neck in neutral alignment, extend your back and hips until your back is nearly straight.

3. Return to the starting position.

Variations: Many variations of this exercise can be done with many types of exercise equipment. You can use a cable column to provide the resistance from a seated position on the floor, or a Roman chair to stabilize the trunk and legs. Regardless of which device you use, avoid hyperextending the spine beyond a straight position.

Trunk Rotation

Focus: Improve core stabilization.

Procedure

1. Sit in the machine with the hips and knees bent 90 degrees.

2. Rotate the trunk in both directions, selecting a range of rotational motion that is comfortable yet simulates the arc of motion you use during your groundstrokes. Move slowly and with control in both directions of this exercise when shortening and lengthening the muscles.

UPPER-BODY EXERCISES

Research has identified significantly greater strength in certain muscles in the tennis player's dominant arm. The muscles most developed through tennis play itself include the internal rotators of the shoulder, biceps and triceps, and forearm muscles. Some players question whether the non-dominant arm should be trained at all because it is not used as much, especially by players who use a one-handed backhand. The following exercises are useful for training the nondominant arm and should be performed, if time allows, to provide greater muscle balance between the left and right arms.

Several of the exercises, such as the Lat Pull-Down and Seated Row, work both arms simultaneously and are excellent for promoting muscle balance of the right and left sides. Even though the amount of time available for strength and conditioning exercises is limited and it is more important to train the rotator cuff and scapular stabilizers on the dominant arm, these exercises could be performed on the nondominant arm when possible, perhaps during the preparation phase of a periodized training program (see chapters 10 and 11).

For a good rotator cuff program, use the exercises described in chapter 11, Solid Shoulder Stability, as part of a comprehensive upper-body strength program:

Sidelying External Rotation (page 172)

Shoulder Extension (page 172)

Prone Horizontal Abduction (page 173)

Prone 90/90 External Rotation (page 174)

Standing External Rotation (page 175)

Standing External Rotation at 90 Degrees of Abduction (page 175)

90/90 Prone Plyometric Ball Drop (page 177)

90/90 Plyometric Reverse Toss (page 178)

Lat Pull-Down

Focus: Improve the strength of the latissimus dorsi, biceps, and scapular stabilizers (rhomboids and trapezius).

Procedure

1. Sit at a lat pull-down machine or sit in a doorway with tubing secured above the door.

2. Grab the lat pull bar with your hands slightly wider than shoulder-width apart or grab the ends of the tubing that are over your head (figure 8.11). Pull the bar down in front of your head to the breast bone or pull the ends of the tubing down, bringing your hands level with your breast bone.

3. Slowly return to the starting position.

Note: Many weight lifters pull down behind the head during this exercise. This is not recommended for tennis players or overhead athletes in general because it places undue stress on the shoulder stabilizers and the joint.

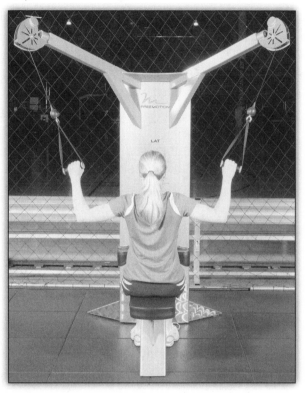

Figure 8.11

Seated Row

DVD

Focus: Improve the strength of the scapular stabilizers (rhomboids and trapezius).

Procedure

1. Sit on a seated row machine or on an exercise ball with tubing anchored at midchest in front of you. (You can also do this exercise from a standing position.)

2. With your hands in front of you, grasp both handles of the machine or the tubing. If you are a standing, assume an athletic posture and engage the muscles of the core by drawing in the abdominals and tensing the gluteal muscles.

3. Keeping your torso upright and looking straight ahead, pull the tubing or handles toward you (figure 8.12). Squeeze your shoulder blades together as your hands come back toward you.

4. Slowly release the weight or tubing to the starting position.

Figure 8.12

Bent-Over Row

Focus: Improve the strength of the scapular stabilizers (rhomboids and trapezius).

Procedure

1. Using a chair or exercise bench for support, use the nonexercising arm and leg to support your body in a bent-over position.

2. Using a dumbbell or exercise tubing or band, begin with the arm fully extended downward. Raise the hand toward your body in a rowing-type motion until it reaches your side (figure 8.13). Squeeze the shoulder blades together as the hand moves toward your side.

Figure 8.13

3. Slowly return to the starting position.

Core Chest Press

Focus: Improve the strength of the upper body.

Procedure

1. Secure one end of tubing or a band at shoulder height. Grab the other end of the tubing and move away from the attachment point until there is tension. Stand holding the tubing in your hand. Face away from the tubing's point of attachment (figure 8.14*a*).

2. Begin with your hand directly at your side and elbow bent 90 degrees. Be sure you are standing in a good athletic position. Engage the core muscles by drawing in the abdominals and tensing the gluteals.

3. Push the hand holding the tubing away from the body until it is fully extended at shoulder height (figure 8.14*b*). Stretch outward at the end of the exercise to move the shoulder blade forward on the upper back. Don't rotate or use the legs or trunk; these should remain stationary.

4. Slowly return to the starting position.

Variation: You can also perform this exercise while holding a dumbbell instead of using the tubing.

Figure 8.14

Biceps Curl

Focus: Improve the strength of the biceps brachii, brachialis, and brachioradialis.

Procedure

1. Stand with your feet shoulder-width apart, a piece of tubing secured underneath your feet. Grasp the handles on the tubing with your palms up.

2. Keeping your upper arms at your sides, bend your elbows and bring the handles toward your shoulders (figure 8.15).

3. If you have chosen the correct tension, you should not have to arch your back or lean back during the exercise.

4. Slowly return to the staring position, making sure you don't hyperextend or lock your elbows.

Variation: You can also perform this exercise while holding dumbbells instead of using the tubing.

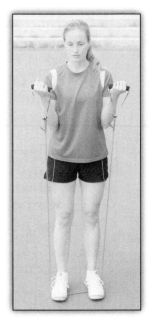

Figure 8.15

Triceps Extension

Focus: Improve the strength of the triceps.

Procedure

1. Lie on your back holding a dumbbell in your hand with your shoulder and elbow bent 90 degrees. Use your opposite hand to support your upper arm and keep it stationary throughout the exercise (figure 8.16).

2. Straighten your elbow by raising your hand and weight upward, making sure the elbow does not lock.

Figure 8.16

FOREARM AND WRIST PROGRAM

Wrist Flexion and Extension

DVD

Focus: Improve the strength of the wrist and finger extensors.

Flexion

1. Sit in a chair with the elbow flexed and forearm resting on a table or over your knee. Hold a light dumbbell in your hand. Let the wrist and hand hang over the edge, with palm facing up.
2. Stabilize the forearm with the opposite hand, and slowly curl your wrist and hand upward (figure 8.17a). Be sure to move only at your wrist, not at your elbow.
3. Raise your hand slowly, hold for a count, and slowly lower the weight.

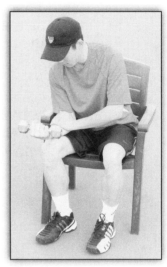

Figure 8.17a

Extension

1. Sit in a chair with the elbow flexed and forearm resting on a table or over your knee. Hold a light dumbbell in your hand. Let the wrist and hand hang over the edge, with the palm facing down.
2. Stabilize the forearm with the opposite hand, and slowly curl your wrist and hand upward (figure 8.17b). Be sure to move only at your wrist, not at your elbow.
3. Raise your hand slowly, hold for a count, and slowly lower the weight.

Figure 8.17b

Radial and Ulnar Deviation

Focus: Improve the strength of the muscles that stabilize the wrist during tennis.

Radial

1. Stand with your arm at your side and grasp a dumbbell on only one end (similar to a hammer). The weighted end should be in front of the thumb.

2. With the wrist in a neutral position and the palm toward the thigh, slowly cock the wrist to raise and lower the weighted end through a comfortable range of motion (figure 8.18*a*). All the movement should occur at the wrist with no elbow or shoulder joint movement. The arc of movement will be small.

Figure 8.18a

Ulnar

1. Stand with your arm at your side and grasp a dumbbell on only one end (similar to a hammer). The weighted end should be behind your little finger.

2. With the wrist in a neutral position and palm facing your thigh, slowly cock the wrist to raise and lower the weighted end through a comfortable range of motion (figure 8.18*b*). All the movement should occur at the wrist with no elbow or shoulder joint movement. The arc of movement will be small.

Figure 8.18b

Pronation and Supination

Focus: Improve the strength of the forearm pronators and supinators.

Forearm Pronation

1. Sit in a chair with the elbow flexed and forearm resting on a table or your knee. Let the wrist and hand hang over the edge.
2. Use a dumbbell with a weight at only one end (similar to a hammer). The weight is on the thumb side to start. Begin the exercise with the palm upward so the handle is horizontal (figure 8.19a). Slowly raise the weighted end by rotating your forearm and wrist until the handle is vertical.
3. Pause for 1 second and return to original start position.

Figure 8.19a

Forearm Supination

1. Sit in a chair with the elbow flexed and forearm resting on a table or your knee. Let the wrist and hand hang over the edge.
2. Use a dumbbell with a weight at only one end (similar to a hammer). The weight should be on the thumb side to start. Begin the exercise with the palm down (figure 8.19b). Slowly raise the weighted ends by rotating your forearm and wrist until the handle is vertical.
3. Pause for 1 second and return to original start position.

Figure 8.19b

Ball Dribble

Focus: Improve the explosive strength of the upper body.

Procedure

1. Holding a small exercise ball or medicine ball, stand 1 to 2 feet (0.3 to 0.6 meters) away from the wall. (How far away you stand from the wall depends on how large the ball is.)

2. Raise your arm to about a 90-degree angle with your torso and rapidly dribble the ball against the wall as fast and explosively as possible for 30 seconds (figure 8.20).

3. The ball will travel just 1 to 2 inches (2.5 to 5 centimeters) away from the wall as you quickly perform the small dribbling motions.

Figure 8.20

SHOULDER PROGRAM

Shrug

Focus: Improve the strength of the upper trapezius and scapular stabilizers.

Procedure

1. Stand with your feet shoulder-width apart and your arms at your sides, grasping dumbbells.

2. Keeping your arms at your sides, raise your shoulders upward toward your ears, then squeeze your shoulder blades together while rolling your shoulders backward.

3. Return to starting position by slowly lowering your shoulders.

Prone Fly

Focus: Improve the strength of the posterior deltoid, rhomboids, and trapezius.

Procedure

1. Lie prone on a narrow bench with your feet off the ground.

2. With dumbbells in hand, extend your arms from your sides at a right angle (90 degrees) with elbows also bent 90 degrees (figure 8.21a).

3. While maintaining a right angle at the shoulders and at the elbow, raise your arms until they are nearly parallel to the ground (figure 8.21b).

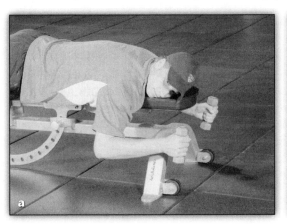

Figure 8.21

Shoulder Punch

Focus: Improve the strength of the serratus anterior, an important scapular stabilizer.

Procedure

1. Lie on your back and hold a small medicine ball or dumbbell.

2. With your arms straight, hold the medicine ball away from your chest. Push the ball toward the ceiling (figure 8.22). Even though your arms are straight, you should be able to push the medicine ball up several inches. This extra motion comes from activation of the serratus anterior, a shoulder blade stabilizer, and the resulting scapular motion it produces.

3. Slowly return to the starting position.

Figure 8.22

PLYOMETRIC MEDICINE BALL PROGRAM

These exercises develop power in the upper body. They use a medicine ball for resistance and require explosive movement patterns. Typically, you can use a 4- to 6-pound (1.8- to 2.7-kilogram) medicine ball. You can increase the weight of the ball when the workout becomes too easy. Begin with sets of 20 to 25 repetitions of each exercise, and advance to performing sets until you fatigue. If you can perform more than 50 repetitions without fatigue, you should increase the weight of the ball.

 ## Plyometric Chest Pass

Focus: Improve the strength of the pectorals, triceps, and scapular stabilizers.

Procedure

1. Stand 8 to 10 feet (2.4 to 3 meters) from a partner. Hold the ball in front of your chest.
2. Pass the ball to your partner. When you receive the ball from your partner, try to catch and release it back to your partner as quickly as possible.

Forehand Toss

Focus: Improve the strength of the muscles used in the forehand.

Procedure

1. Stand 8 to 10 feet (2.4 to 3 meters) from your partner. Hold the ball with both hands at your forehand side.
2. Step and turn, just as you would to hit your forehand, taking the ball back like a racket. Pass the ball to your partner, mimicking a crosscourt forehand groundstroke.
3. When you receive the ball from your partner, try to catch and release it back to your partner as quickly as possible.

Backhand Toss

Focus: Improve the strength of the muscles used in the backhand.

Procedure

1. Stand 8 to 10 feet (2.4 to 3 meters) from your partner. Hold the ball with both hands at your backhand side.

2. Step and turn, just as you would to hit your backhand, taking the ball back like a racket. Pass the ball to your partner, mimicking a crosscourt backhand groundstroke.

3. When you receive the ball from your partner, try to catch and release it back to your partner as quickly as possible.

SUMMARY

The resistive exercises and concepts discussed in this chapter are key to developing a successful tennis-specific strength and conditioning program. Adhering to the guidelines and recommendations in this chapter and integrating them with the material presented in other chapters with area-specific guidelines will enable you to perform safe and effective exercises to enhance performance and prevent injury.

Chapter 9

Aerobic and Anaerobic Training

Optimal tennis performance requires a combination of high-intensity, powerful bursts of activity, such as serve-and-volley sequences or running wide to cover a crosscourt groundstoke, and the stamina and endurance to repeatedly perform these activities over a match lasting several hours or a grueling practice session. The intense physical demands in the modern game of tennis require tennis players to possess high levels of both aerobic and anaerobic fitness. As mentioned previously, match analyses indicate that 300 to 500 bursts of energy are required over the course of a tennis match that can last for 2 to 3 hours. To design a program that addresses a player's aerobic and anaerobic fitness, it is important to understand the general concepts and inherent characteristics of the anaerobic and aerobic energy systems.

TENNIS: AN AEROBIC AND ANAEROBIC SPORT

Research performed on tennis players during singles practice and match play has consistently rated tennis as a prolonged moderate-intensity exercise activity. One indicator used by exercise scientists and medical doctors to measure exercise intensity is heart rate. Activities are rated as a percentage of a person's maximal heart rate. Maximal heart rate can be measured directly by performing a treadmill or bicycle ergometer maximal stress test that incrementally increases the exercise intensity until the athlete cannot continue. The heart rate in beats per minute at the time of exhaustion from the exercise workload is the maximal heart rate. When scientific testing is not practical, maximal heart rate value can be estimated using the following equation:

maximal heart rate = 220 − athlete's age

Using the formula for a 20-year-old tennis player would result in a maximal heart rate of 200 beats per minute. Exercise intensities would then be expressed as a percentage of the maximal heart rate.

Research conducted on tennis players in most studies shows the intensity level to range between 60 and 90 percent of maximum heart rate. This means that for the 20-year-old player, heart rate would range from 120 to 180 beats per minute during tennis play. This heart rate intensity classifies tennis as an activity that meets the requirement of the American College of Sports Medicine for improving cardiovascular fitness.

Tennis play consists of repeated high-intensity bouts of exertion while maintaining a moderate overall intensity throughout performance. Therefore, it poses both aerobic and anaerobic demands. Figure 9.1 displays common sport activities that require a combination of aerobic and anaerobic energy and shows where they fall on the aerobic–anaerobic continuum.

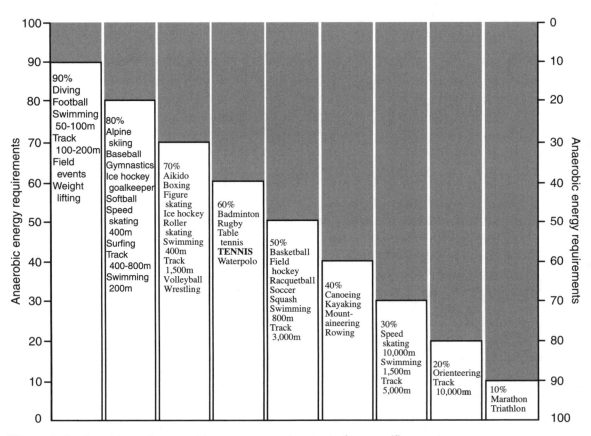

Figure 9.1 Aerobic and anaerobic energy requirements for specific sports.

Adapted by permission from B. Sharkey, 1985, *Coaches Guide to Sport Physiology* (Champaign, IL: Human Kinetics), 100.

TENNIS: A CONTINUUM OF ANAEROBIC AND AEROBIC ENERGY PRODUCTION

Based on the physiological activity patterns of tennis play, a player must develop both aerobic and anaerobic fitness to play at his or her highest level. What exactly does anaerobic and aerobic fitness mean?

Anaerobic means *without oxygen* and refers to two of the energy systems used by the body to produce energy units called adenosine triphosphate (ATP). ATP is required for virtually every activity the body performs, whether breathing, contracting the heart, or engaging muscles to hit a backhand.

Anaerobic energy production, or metabolism, involves two systems. The first and most immediate is the ATP-PC system, which consists of stored energy within the muscles and working tissues. Limited amounts of ATP can be produced by this anaerobic system, only enough to fuel 6 to 10 seconds of maximal-intensity work (see figure 9.2).

After approximately 10 seconds of intense work, the predominant energy system used by the body is termed *anaerobic glycolysis*. Glycolysis involves breaking down the carbohydrate taken in by the body from the diet through a complex chemical process and conversion. This process produces ATP. A by-product of anaerobic glycolysis is lactic acid, which is formed during the production of ATP using this system. Eventually with continued high-intensity work by the muscle, lactic acid begins to accumulate in the muscle, and the athlete is forced to stop because of the burning sensation within the muscle caused by the lactic acid.

Anaerobic glycolysis is only an effective energy source for high-intensity exercise lasting 2 to 3 minutes. At that time, exercise activity must either

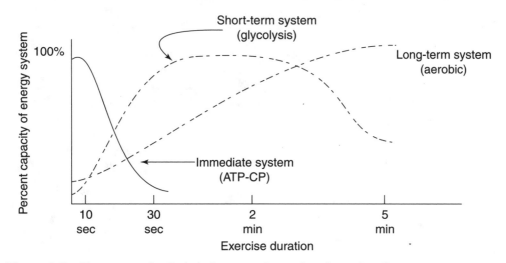

Figure 9.2 Energy production during exercises of various durations.

Reprinted by permission from McArdle, Katch, and Katch, 1981, *Exercise Physiology: Energy, Nutrition, and Human Performance* (Philadelphia: Lea and Febiger), 134.

stop or become less intense to allow the next energy system to step in and produce energy for more prolonged activity. This final energy system is the aerobic energy system. The aerobic energy system takes in oxygen through the lungs and carries it to the working tissues in the bloodstream. In the presence of adequate amounts of oxygen, the aerobic energy system is a highly efficient producer of ATP and is the primary energy system relied on for long, endurance-oriented sport activities, such as running a 10K or a marathon.

TENNIS AND ENERGY SYSTEMS

Applying the energy system continuum to tennis is easy and helps illustrate the reason that both anaerobic and aerobic conditioning is necessary for enhancing tennis performance. Because tennis ultimately involves repetitive muscular contractions and exertion, the aerobic energy system provides the baseline energy production over the duration of a tennis match or practice session. Aerobic fitness is also important for recovery following a strenuous baseline rally, bursts of movement, and maximal skills such as executing a serve-and-volley sequence or an overhead.

Anaerobic energy production is required for maximal activities during points. Testing, in the form of treadmill tests and endurance runs, performed by the United States Tennis Association (USTA) on elite tennis players indicates high levels of aerobic fitness. Sprinting and agility tests indicate superior anaerobic power. This explains a player's ability to maximally sprint from side to side during a baseline rally, and after 20 to 25

Kim Clijsters attacks the ball during a rally. Tennis requires both aerobic and anaerobic endurance for long rallies and short bursts of speed.

seconds rest, do it again. Athletes with better aerobic fitness levels can clear the accumulated lactic acid from the working muscles more rapidly than players with less aerobic fitness. Likewise, athletes with greater aerobic power can run faster and jump higher because of greater energy stores in the trained muscle.

TENNIS TRAINING FOR ANAEROBIC POWER

Analysis of tennis matches generally determines that the average point lasts approximately 10 seconds. Average rest taken by most players is 18 to 20 seconds, with a maximum allowable rest time between points being 25 seconds. This creates what is called a work-to-rest cycle. A 1:2 work-to-rest cycle is most representative of the physiological activity pattern experienced during tennis. In addition to the work-to-rest cycle concept, the term *specificity* is often applied. Specificity involves training the athlete in a manner most similar to the actual demands of his or her sport.

Anaerobic training techniques in tennis use both the work-to-rest and specificity concepts. Drills and activities used to improve anaerobic power follow the 1:2 work-to-rest cycle and include relatively short, multidirectional movement patterns. Listed below are characteristics of tennis play that can be incorporated into tennis-specific training:

Characteristics Addressed in Specificity

- A tennis point usually includes four or five directional changes.
- Most tennis points last fewer than 10 seconds.
- Tennis players always carry their racket during points.
- Players seldom run more than 30 feet (9 meters) in one direction during a point.
- Movement patterns contain acceleration and controlled deceleration.

Tennis-specific drills to improve on-court movement and footwork as well as anaerobic power are included in chapters 5 and 6. Any exercise that includes a relatively short period of maximal-intensity work followed by a period of recovery that is approximately two times longer than the period of work stresses the anaerobic energy system. General anaerobic training drills for tennis include classic on-court movement drills such as wind sprints and line drills and the side shuffle, alley hop, and kangaroo hop. Perform all of these general anaerobic training drills with a tennis racket in hand (just like you do when you are playing) to make the drills more specific to tennis.

A tennis-specific anaerobic training drill is described as follows and charted in table 9.1. It was adapted from Loehr in the USTA *Sport Science for Tennis Newsletter*, spring, 1991.

Table 9.1   Work (W)/Rest (R) Interval Schedule

Feed	Series 1 W/R	Series 2 W/R	Series 3 W/R	Series 4 W/R	Series 5 W/R
1	2/15	7/20	8/20	3/25	7/20
2	6/15	2/20	8/20	3/25	5/20
3	3/15	2/20	8/20	3/25	1/20
4	10/15	16/20	8/20	3/25	10/20
5	8/15	4/20	8/20	3/25	6/20
6	2/15	6/20	8/20	3/25	3/20
7	7/15	1/20	8/20	3/25	2/20
8	15/15	12/20	8/20	3/25	7/20
9	4/15	9/20	8/20	3/25	16/20
10	3/15	3/20	8/20	3/25	4/20

W is the number of balls to feed (work); R is the number of seconds of recovery (rest).

Feeds 6 through 10 should occur in each series only after the player has served the ball.

Player takes a 90-second sit-down break between each series. During the 90-second break, the feeder must pick up the balls and prepare for the next series. The feeder must also record heart rates before and after the break.

Whenever possible, record the number of balls hit outside the designated target areas. The goal is to keep errors to a minimum during all sequences.

Adapted, by permission, from Loehr, USTA *Sport Science for Tennis Newsletter,* Spring 1991, White Plains, NY: USTA, 4.

1. Get a hitting partner or coach to feed you balls. One coach can conduct this training sequence for a maximum of two players at once.

2. Each player will be drilled for 1 hour. If you have a hitting partner, alternate every 30 minutes; you will need a 2-hour time block.

3. Provide a minimum of 80 balls per player; 160 balls are needed if a coach is working with two players.

4. Get a stopwatch.

5. Use realistic feeding. Remember the average distance covered per point is only 60 feet (18 meters); therefore, feeding continuously from corner to corner is unrealistic. Feeding rate should be approximately 1.3 seconds per feed. At that rate, feeding 15 balls should take about 20 seconds. The feeder can vary the placement of the balls based on the needs of the player. A waist-high ball basket will assist the coach with feeding. The player should not know how many balls will be fed during each point, thus simulating match situations.

6. Place targets such as cones, ball cans, or boxes on the court. These designate hitting areas.

7. Hit balls at designated target areas.

8. Except for the warm-up, complete the entire series at maximum intensity.

9. The feeder follows a predetermined schedule of exercise and rest intervals spaced every 10 to 15 minutes, with 90-second breaks for you to sit down, drink, and towel off. You must sit down during these breaks.

10. Use a heart rate monitor (optional). Take heart rates before and after 90-second breaks to gauge workloads, intensity levels, and recovery rates.

AEROBIC TRAINING FOR TENNIS

For an exercise activity to stress the aerobic system, you must adhere to several basic concepts. Aerobic exercise training activities typically involve major muscle groups, are repetitive in nature, and include continuous exertion in repeated or cycled fashion. Examples of aerobic activities are running, swimming, stair-climbing, sliding, and biking. Additional characteristics of aerobic exercise include frequency, duration, and intensity. The American College of Sports Medicine provides the following general guidelines for improving aerobic fitness through exercise:

Duration: minimum of 20 minutes of continuous exercise

Frequency: minimum of three times per week

Intensity: 60 to 85 percent of maximum heart rate

Improving and maintaining aerobic fitness levels are important parts of the overall training program for tennis players. Identify players with low levels of aerobic fitness using the fitness testing guidelines outlined in chapter 3.

Include aerobic exercise depending on the degree of need in the player's training program. When adding aerobic training to a player's program, consider several factors. One factor is timing. Do not fatigue a player by scheduling aerobic exercise before a skill-oriented practice session. Aerobic training should be done after skill-oriented, tennis-specific training and on light training days.

Just as you would with other types of exercise training, start aerobic training gradually, once or twice a week along with other training activities. Progress based on the athlete's needs. Additionally, choose an aerobic training activity that best suits the player. If a player has a history of knee or another lower-extremity injury, adding distance running to his or her training program may not be as appropriate as cycling, sliding on a slideboard (or other lateral-movement exercise), or swimming. Use the cross-training concept with aerobic training to prevent boredom, encourage multiple muscle group development, and increase enjoyment. Use testing to measure aerobic fitness levels and gauge improvement. Excessive aerobic training may invite overuse injuries and take precious training time away from anaerobic and skill-oriented tennis training.

SUMMARY

To perform optimally on court requires high levels of both aerobic and anaerobic fitness. Neither of these important factors should be neglected in a complete conditioning program for tennis. Testing, retesting, and tracking changes and improvements in the player's fitness levels can serve as an excellent guide for determining how much training in each of these areas to include during a player's training cycle. Use varied and creative formats to enhance both aerobic and anaerobic fitness levels and incorporate the specificity principles outlined in this chapter.

Chapter 10

Program Design

What is the best way to train the body for tennis? Most people approach training with a "if some is good, more is better" philosophy. If a little strength training will improve power, then more will improve power to an even greater extent. A player may also say, "I've seen tremendous improvements in my game while practicing five days a week. If I practice every day, I will become even better." Although these sentiments seem to make sense, they are not necessarily true.

It's been said that strength training and conditioning are not rocket science, and in fact there are several ways players can improve strength and fitness, such as using free weights or machines or engaging in regular conditioning sessions. However, physical training is actually a complex science. Think of the complexity of the human body. If a player wants to optimize performance gains in tennis, it is best to work with these systems and not against them.

Two principles govern how the body responds to exercise:

1. Specific adaptation to imposed demands (SAID principle). This principle states that the body will respond, and adapt, to the demands that are placed on it. Simply put, if you train by lifting heavier weights or performing more explosive exercises, your body will respond by becoming stronger or more powerful, respectively. This sounds great—all you have to do is lift more weight or complete more training and the body will respond. But you also need to consider the second principle.

2. General adaptation syndrome (GAS principle). The GAS principle states that training effects do not occur overnight, and in fact, the body adapts gradually over time, if given adequate time to rest and recover. The body needs time to recover from the stress you put on it. For example, after a stressful day at the office, you are likely to come

home agitated, tired, and in need of rest in order to regenerate for the next day. The same is true for physical training; your muscles, hormonal systems, bones, and so on need time to recover following a period of stress, like a training session.

Taken together, these two principles can be used to shape the quantity and intensity of training for tennis. More often than not, the recovery portion of the equation is missed, resulting in players who train or compete in a less-than-optimal state. Incorporating this balance between work and rest is the foundation of what we call *periodization training*.

PERIODIZATION TRAINING

Periodization is the systematic process of structuring training and competition into phases to maximize an athlete's chances of achieving peak performances. Periodization typically involves a training plan that includes specified periods devoted to building general fitness and muscular endurance, high intensity training, competition, and rest. When structured appropriately, a periodized training program can optimize a player's performance gains and help a tennis player peak at the most important times of the season. Most important, incorporating active rest into the periodized

Amelie Mauresmo returns the ball from the baseline. Periodized training prepares the athlete to peak when maximum performance is needed.

training model helps to prevent the injury, burnout, and fatigue that can lead to impaired performance.

Think about your own tennis training and what has produced the best results for you in the past. When you do the same thing every day—the same exercises, the same weights, the same intensity—it does not take long before things get boring or stale. If you are like most people, you likely will lose interest pretty quickly. The body likes variation, and the muscles and cardiorespiratory system respond in much the same way as the mind. When things get repetitive, the body tunes out and stops making gains.

Another important aspect of periodized training is specificity, which means matching the training to the demands of the sport and being intentional about what you do. Every training session, whether on the court or in the weight room, should have a specific focus and intensity. Additionally, every training session should be seen as an opportunity to improve in some way, whether it is a physical or tactical skill for tennis. When you think of what a tennis player needs for top performance, it is easy to assemble quite a list of attributes that are needed to be successful on the court—endurance, strength, flexibility, power, coordination, and the list goes on.

History of Periodization

Although the concept of periodized training is relatively new to tennis, the concept of alternating periods of intense training and rest with the goal of peaking for important competitions was first used by the Greeks during the Olympic Games of the ancient era. The foundations of modern periodized principles, however, were laid in the former Soviet Union in the early part of the 20th century. Although periodized training has been used for some time in other sports, strength and conditioning experts have less information available to guide the development of a periodized program for tennis. One study followed collegiate female tennis players over a 9-month training period. One group of players performed a periodized resistive-exercise program using multiple sets of exercise, while another group performed a nonperiodized resistive-exercise program using one set of exercise.

> **CONDITIONING TIP**
>
> Multiple sets of resistance training provide better results than single sets of training.

This detailed study showed that throughout the training program, the group of female players performing the periodized, multiple-set training program experienced greater gains in muscular strength, power, and endurance and greater improvements in body composition and on-court tennis performance. This study provides valuable evidence in favor of the use of periodized training programs that are specifically designed for tennis players.

Traditional Periodized Training

Most books and articles on periodization will tell you that a well-designed plan should include a preparation phase, a precompetitive phase, a competitive phase, and an active rest phase.

Preparation Phase

The focus of the preparation phase is on developing a base level of fitness and strength, what we'll call foundational conditioning and strength. The training goals of the preparation phase include the following:

- Challenge the aerobic energy system, for example, 20 to 40 minutes of aerobic training at 70 to 85 percent of maximum heart rate three or four times per week.
- Establish a strength base, for example, strength training using a high-repetition (10 to 15 repetitions per set for 2 or 3 sets), low-resistance training program.
- Include technical and tactical training, for example, on-court training that incorporates changes in stroke mechanics, develops new shots, and so on.

Precompetitive Phase

The precompetitive phase is a period leading up to the competitive season in which the training shifts from general training to training for power and activities more closely related to the demands of the sport. In the precompetitive phase, the intensity level increases, and the goals become more tennis specific:

- Challenge the anaerobic energy system, for example, on-court training drills and interval training using tennis-specific work-to-rest intervals.
- Improve speed and power, for example, sprinting and explosive on-court exercises and plyometrics.
- Improve muscular strength, for example, perform 2 to 4 sets with 8 to 10 repetitions, decrease the training volume, and increase the intensity of the resistance exercise.
- Maintain aerobic status, for example, perform aerobic exercise two times per week for 20 to 30 minutes.
- Improve tennis-specific skill, for example, on-court training focused on tennis-specific drills, practice matches, and simulated points in preparation for competition.

Competitive Phase

During the competitive phase, players should maintain their conditioning and strength over a period of competitions or peak for a specific competition. Here again, training goals are sport specific:

- Maintain peak performance.
- Keep workout intensity high.
- Participate in tennis competitions or tennis-specific training.

Active Rest Phase

During the active rest phase, the athlete takes a mental and physical break from the sport. This is not a time for the athlete to do nothing, however, but is a time to cross-train:

- Rest from tennis.
- Participate in other activities to maintain fitness levels.
- Emphasize fun, low-intensity workouts.
- Rest for 1 to 4 weeks.

This periodized structure works well for sports with well-defined seasons and off-seasons, but what about tennis? Tennis has no real off-season, and competitions occur almost every weekend throughout the year. Does this training model have a place in tennis?

Andy Roddick diving to make the shot. Although tennis is a year-round sport, periodization principles still apply.

PERIODIZATION TRAINING FOR TENNIS

The quick answer to the question of whether tennis players can benefit from periodized training is "yes!" However, several factors make periodized training more difficult in tennis compared to other sports. It is important to recognize these obstacles and acknowledge that they exist before identifying ways to get around them.

- Tennis is a year-round sport, which for most players has no well-defined preseason or off-season. Tennis players do not have the luxury of peaking once every four years, like athletes in Olympic sports, or even several times per year, like players in many other sports. Tennis players feel the need to be ready to compete at a high level week in and week out. How do you incorporate preseason and off-season training into a training plan if such seasons don't exist in tennis?

- A player competing in a tournament does not know when he or she is going to lose. A player can lose in the first round or advance to the finals. This makes it difficult to plan a training schedule in advance.

- Tennis tends to reward more successful players, allowing them more time to recover between peak performances. Top professional players have the luxury of being able to skip events and still win enough money to make a living or earn ranking points. Similarly, top junior players do not have to chase points across the country or around the world. The players who are trying to make it to the next level feel they have to play more to earn ranking points and consequently have little or no downtime between events.

Even in light of these factors, periodization is still important for tennis players. However, training must be approached a bit differently than it is by football players, swimmers, or soccer players.

Obstacles in Tennis

Tennis is a tough sport to train for. It would be great if all a player had to do to optimize his or her fitness, conditioning, and strength was to practice hitting balls and compete. Unfortunately, many players take this approach and never realize that they are selling themselves short and are not reaching their full potential.

A player will never completely recognize his or her full potential without structured strength and conditioning training. Why bring this point up here, in a chapter on periodization? Because following a periodized training plan means that a player may have to sacrifice short-term gains in exchange for greater rewards and improved performance down the road. Periodized training requires that you develop a preseason in which you work on building fitness, strength, power, or whatever attributes are key to your game. This may mean training through some tournaments, when you know you may not be at your best.

The upside is that when other players are getting injured late in the season or are becoming fatigued, you can draw on the fitness and strength you developed earlier in the year. You are also setting the stage for success years down the road. Contrary to popular belief, an 18-year-old who advances from the junior to the professional ranks without engaging in a strength and conditioning program cannot expect his or her body to transform overnight and be able to compete with adults. Strength training and conditioning must be a part of a developing player's tennis training from early on, and that will make the transition to a higher age group, or even the professional ranks, easier. Let's look at the three main obstacles that face tennis players and discuss possible ways to counter them.

Length of the Season

A player will be best served if he or she can devote time within the competitive season, ideally 6 to 8 weeks, to focus on building a base of fitness and strength. Although the player can still compete during this time, he or she should recognize that performance may be less than optimal. However, this base will allow the player to improve in the areas of fitness or strength and serve as the foundation from which the player will draw late in the season when other players are faltering. This is the time when players will do high volumes of work—high repetitions with low weights—and work hard to build cardiorespiratory endurance.

Not Knowing When the Tournament Will End

This is a tough one because every week can be different. However, recognize that strength and conditioning training does not necessarily require a weight room or fancy equipment. The United States Tennis Association encourages players to travel with equipment, such as stretch tubing, a small medicine ball, several cones for movement drills, and a plan for what will happen if they lose in the first round or the second round or make it to the finals so they can start training without missing a beat. Remember when you aren't maintaining or improving fitness or strength, you are losing it. Some estimates of cardiorespiratory fitness show that you need two days of training to make up for the deficits induced by taking one day off from your regular training plan. So plan for any scenario, and be prepared to train at an event if necessary.

Lack of Rest for Players Chasing Money or Ranking Points

Rest is key for any player, and it is important to incorporate it into your training plan. Players who train or compete day after day with no breaks, don't give their bodies a chance to recover, adapt, or grow. We typically recommend that in a 7-day training week, one day be devoted to complete rest with little or no intense physical activity, and one day involve active rest. Active rest means doing something other than playing tennis or training for tennis in the weight room or through on-court conditioning. So, once a week go for a bike ride, play soccer, swim, or do something that still involves activity but relieves the body of the stresses it experiences when training for tennis.

Additionally, players need a period, or periods, during the year away from serious tennis training. Again, this is a time for recovery from the demands of a competitive season, a phase of intense training, and so on. This provides not only a physical break but a mental break, allowing players to recharge the battery. This is another one of those things that seems counterintuitive, especially for a player who feels the need to compete every week to earn every conceivable ranking point. But think about it. What happens to the quality of your play when you have no time to recharge or rest? Similarly, don't you feel recharged after taking a short break from the sport? Doesn't your attitude, intensity, and focus improve after a vacation? (The same holds true for your work or study performance, too.) Is it coincidence that several top professional players have elevated the level of their game after rehabilitating from an injury and giving their body a chance to rest and recover? Likely it is not a

Martina Hingis reaches for the ball on clay. Plan ahead for training during tournaments and bring simple equipment, such as tubing, with you on the road.

coincidence. Do not short change yourself on rest; it pays great dividends down the road.

Rest is a vital part of any training plan and is a necessity for any athlete, tennis players included, to reach his or her full potential. It is easy for a tennis player to become overtrained, a phenomenon exemplified by sluggishness, tiredness, and feelings of apathy, because of all the training players typically engage in. Although this is especially true for high-performance players, it is also possible for recreational players to fall into this trap, especially if they are rededicating themselves to fitness or training and making drastic changes to their training plan.

Training Specificity

Training specificity refers to how well training matches the physical and physiological demands of the sport. As a general rule, the closer you get to an important competition or a series of competitions you hope to peak for, the more your training should match the demands of the game. During the time in which you are building a base of strength and fitness, the exercises can be nonspecific. However, the intensity and types of exercises should change as you get closer to your main competitive season. Examples follow.

Strength

When developing a strength and fitness base, perform a high number of repetitions of exercises using weights light enough that you can perform 3 sets of 15 to 20 repetitions. Exercises can include many of the traditional weight room exercises to build strength—Bench Press, Squat, Lunge, Lat Pull-Down—but stay away from overhead lifting.

Once you get closer to the in-season, or competitive, phase, you will increase training specificity and incorporate exercises that involve the entire body and multiple planes of motion, including rotation. These exercises should engage the entire kinetic chain and incorporate movements similar to those seen in tennis. The number of repetitions will decrease, and the amount of weight will increase. Additionally, you should increase the intensity by adding more sets. An example is performing 4 sets of 4 repetitions of a Partial Squat with a medicine ball.

Power

Early in the periodized training cycle, do not focus on developing power. Power means generating force quickly, and you need to build a base level of strength first. Engage in low-level plyometrics early on, but as you get closer to the competitive season, shift your emphasis to more and more exercises that develop explosiveness and power, which are required on the tennis court. Exercises that emphasize power also require increased rest. Take several minutes between sets to ensure high quality.

Cardiorespiratory Fitness

As the season progresses, long, slow distance training, which can be used to build a base of cardiorespiratory fitness, should give way to endurance training that incorporates interval training with work-to-rest ratios similar to what a player experiences in tennis (1:2 to 1:3). For example, perform a movement drill for 10 seconds and take 20 to 30 seconds of rest.

Sample Periodized Plan for Tennis

A player could structure a season in many ways in terms of the number of tournaments to play and the times at which he or she wants to peak during the year. Keep in mind the guidelines set forth earlier for how much time to dedicate to each phase of training and the ability to peak.

The periodized training program shown in figure 10.1 is designed for a player who wants to peak twice in a year. Maybe it is an elite junior player who wants to peak for the International Spring Championships in the spring and the U.S. Open Junior Tennis Championships in late summer. Maybe it is an adult league player who hopes to perform his or her best at the country club spring and summer championships. Although the specific exercises and weights used may differ between these two players, the overall structure of their plans will be similar. Pay attention to the following:

- Training volume should be high in the preparation phase, and intensity should be low to moderate.
- In the precompetition phase, the training shifts to lower volumes, but higher intensity.
- During competition, the volume should be very low, but the intensity should be high. Matches count as high-intensity exercise. Also, players should not be afraid to train during a tournament. Many of the exercises presented in this book can be done on the road.
- During the active rest phase, volume and intensity decrease.

This diagram shows one possibility for structuring the season; however, it is not the only way. You see that even within a phase, the volume and intensity fluctuate somewhat to provide varied stimuli to the body while also allowing times to recover.

Plan your schedule by first identifying the main tournaments you want to peak for, identifying preparation and precompetition phases, and then varying the volume and intensity of the work within each phase.

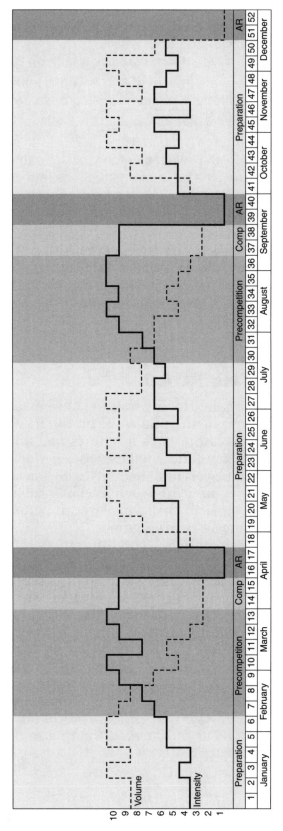

Figure 10.1　Sample periodization training program for a tennis player who wants to peak once in the spring and once in the summer.

BUILDING YOUR PERIODIZED TRAINING PLAN

1. Start by identifying the most important tournaments on the calendar.

2. Identify a period (or several periods) of 6 to 8 weeks that you are willing to devote to building a strength and conditioning base.

3. Identify a period (or several periods) that you will take off from tennis for an active rest phase.

4. Develop a chart or table and select an emphasis for each week of the year. For example, during the base-strength phase, the emphasis may be on building endurance. However, 2 weeks before the main competition, the emphasis may be on maximizing power or improving on-court movement.

5. Become even more detailed, and outline exercises, sets, and repetitions for each day. You do not have to lay out every day of the year on January 1, but some foresight should go into your planning, and you should know what you are going to do several weeks or months down the line.

TRAINING ON THE ROAD

Changes in strength and conditioning training have made it much easier for tennis players to continue training while on the road. These changes have included a shift away from large machines traditionally housed in gyms and training centers to functional exercises performed on court or virtually anywhere tennis players find themselves. By traveling with several easily portable pieces of equipment—such as elastic tubing and bands, a foam pad, cones, and a medicine ball—players can perform nearly every exercise in this book while away from home.

Another key aspect of strength and conditioning training while on the road is the lack of time available for training while traveling. Therefore a periodized model is essential for providing an organized and systematically varied program that can be carried out over an extended period. For example, while traveling between tournaments, players typically perform fewer strength and conditioning exercises because of the increased emphasis on tennis-specific, on-court training. However, by using elastic tubing and other portable exercise equipment, players can maintain key strength relationships in the shoulder and upper back or continue working on the hip and core muscles, making the most of their limited time. Targeting the areas of need identified through the testing protocol outlined in chapter 3 is an excellent way to focus on-the-road training in light of the time limitations typically encountered.

SUMMARY

Although tennis is a year-round sport, the concept of periodization training is no less important for tennis players than it is for other athletes. In fact, by properly structuring training and competition into phases, players maximize their chances of peaking at the desired times. A solid program design focuses on the long-term benefits of training, not just immediate results. The previous chapters (and exercises on the DVD) each focused on specific components of a well-designed training program. Planning and organizing these components into a periodized training schedule will allow you to improve your performance at the desired times.

Chapter 11

Solid Shoulder Stability

The shoulder is one of the most frequently injured areas in elite-level tennis players; the stresses on the shoulder are repetitive and can easily lead to overuse injuries if proper technique and strength are not maintained. Yet, many of these injuries can be prevented by engaging in a strength and conditioning program that targets the muscles of the shoulder and upper back. An understanding of the basic structure and function of the shoulder is important for any tennis player or coach. This chapter provides this information and also presents specific exercises that can be used to prevent injury to this critical link in the kinetic chain.

BASIC SHOULDER ANATOMY AND STRUCTURE

The actual shoulder joint, also known as the glenohumeral joint, is best described as a ball and socket. The head of the humerus, the bone in the upper arm, makes the "ball," and it fits into the "socket," which is called the glenoid fossa, on the shoulder blade. This arrangement makes the shoulder one of the most mobile joints in the human body. However, the structure of the shoulder also makes it susceptible to injury. Unlike other joints in the body, the shoulder has few ligaments to provide support; a thin joint capsule provides a small amount of overall stability to the joint. The main stabilizing forces in the shoulder are provided by muscles. The most important stabilizers are the four muscles that make up the rotator cuff (see figure 11.1): the supraspinatus, infraspinatus, subscapularis, and teres minor. These muscles help with shoulder movement but also are important for pulling the ball into the socket. Weakness in these muscles, which is common in tennis players, can lead to early fatigue, altered technique, and ultimately injury.

In addition to providing stability to the shoulder joint, specific muscles of the rotator cuff contract concentrically to provide powerful internal rotation, the motion a tennis player uses to hit a forehand and accelerate forward to contact the ball on the serve. Other rotator cuff muscles contract eccentrically to provide the critical arm deceleration following ball contact on the serve. This deceleration of the arm can be stressful to tendons and is one of the main reasons the rotator cuff tendons become overloaded and injured with repetitive tennis play.

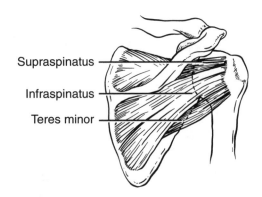

Figure 11.1 Back view of the shoulder showing the supraspinatus and infraspinatus in the rotator cuff.

CHARACTERISTICS OF THE TENNIS PLAYER'S SHOULDER

It would be natural to think that because of all the balls a player hits, the shoulder muscles in a tennis player's dominant (tennis playing) arm would be much stronger than those in the nondominant arm. In fact, some of the muscles, those that internally rotate the shoulder, are very strong. In the modern game of tennis, as much as 75 percent of all shots are forehands and serves. These shots involve a great deal of internal rotation and strengthen these muscles quite a bit.

However, research has shown that the muscles that externally rotate the shoulder (bring the arm back) can actually be weaker in the tennis-playing arm. This phenomenon is common in tennis players and likely results from the stress placed on these muscles during the follow-through of the service motion, where the muscle works eccentrically (lengthens during contraction). This repetitive stress can overload the muscles and cause tendon breakdown. It then becomes a vicious cycle, as the breakdown contributes to greater weakness, which then places the tennis player's shoulder at an even greater risk for injury. The decreased strength in these important muscles further compromises proper joint function.

The discrepancy between the strong internal rotators and the weak external rotators creates a strength and muscle imbalance in the shoulder. It has been likened to having a sports car in the front of the shoulder (internal rotators) and an old jalopy in the back (external rotators). If left unaddressed, this imbalance can lead to improper tracking of the shoulder joint and possibly injury.

Many players and coaches ask, "Doesn't playing tennis simply strengthen these muscles? Isn't that all the training I need?" The answer is no. Research has shown that simply playing tennis does not adequately strengthen the muscles in the back of the shoulder. In an attempt to restore balance to the shoulder, players need to engage in tennis-specific exercises that focus on strengthening the muscles that externally rotate the shoulder as well as the muscles in the upper back that stabilize the shoulder blade.

Another adaptation seen in the shoulders of many tennis players is the ability to externally rotate the arm farther than a normal shoulder can (see figure 11.2). This increased flexibility into external rotation, coupled with the fact that the tennis player's shoulder can be unstable, has led therapists to label tennis players as having a "Gumby shoulder," like the bendable rubber cartoon character. Because of this looseness and increased flexibility in external rotation, players and coaches are cautioned against performing additional stretches of these muscles. Placing the arms behind the body and forcibly stretching the shoulder in external rotation was a common practice among tennis players and baseball pitchers years ago, but it is not recommended today based on what we now know.

Figure 11.2 Sam Querrey demonstrates maximum external rotation during the tennis serve.

Although tennis players frequently show increased flexibility in shoulder external rotation in the dominant arm, research also shows that players tend to have flexibility deficits in the opposite direction—internal rotation—compared to the nondominant arm. This lost internal rotation likely comes from the repetitive overuse of certain shoulder muscles and joint structures, resulting in chronic tightness in the muscles in the back of the shoulder. The loss of internal rotation seems to increase with the amount of tennis a person plays and actually creates harmful movements inside the shoulder that can lead to injury. Tennis players should have their shoulder flexibility measured by a physical therapist or trainer to identify flexibility deficits in internal rotation. These health care professionals can recommend stretches to increase internal rotation range of motion.

SHOULDER INJURIES IN TENNIS

Interestingly, the most common injury site in the shoulder is not the rotator cuff muscles themselves but rather the tendons that attach these muscles to the upper arm. There is not a lot of space inside the shoulder. When muscles fatigue or improper technique is used, it is very easy for one of the rotator cuff tendons that pass through this space to get pinched. When this happens over and over again, it can lead to tendinitis. Many of the shoulder injuries seen in tennis can be prevented with a proper stretching and strengthening program.

STRETCHES TO PREVENT SHOULDER INJURIES

The two most important shoulder stretches for tennis players are the Cross-Arm Stretch and the Sleeper Stretch. Research shows that using these stretches as part of a regular program will improve the range of motion of internal rotation.

PREVENTIVE SHOULDER STRETCHES

As with any stretch, perform them after tennis play and complete two or three repetitions of each stretch, holding each for 20 to 30 seconds. This will improve or maintain flexibility in the shoulder.

Cross-Arm Stretch

Focus: Improve the flexibility of the muscles in the back of the shoulder and back of the shoulder joint capsule.

Procedure

1. Stand next to a doorway or fence, if possible. Raise your racket arm to shoulder level. Brace the side of your shoulder and shoulder blade against the wall or fence to keep the shoulder blade from sliding forward when you begin the stretch.

2. Using the other hand, grab the outside of the elbow of your racket hand and pull your arm across your chest (figure 11.3). You should feel the stretch in the back of your shoulder.

Note: If you feel a pinching sensation in the front of your shoulder, discontinue this stretch and use the Sleeper Stretch to accomplish a similar stretch for this portion of the shoulder.

Figure 11.3

Sleeper Stretch

DVD

Focus: Improve the flexibility of the muscles in the back of the shoulder and back of the shoulder joint capsule.

Procedure

1. Lie on your dominant shoulder in a position you might adopt when sleeping on your side (hence the name).
2. Place your dominant arm directly in front of you, with the elbow bent 90 degrees.
3. Using your other arm, push your hand down toward your feet, internally rotating your shoulder (figure 11.4).
4. Hold for 20 to 30 seconds.

Figure 11.4

STRENGTHENING EXERCISES TO PREVENT SHOULDER INJURIES

Increasing muscular endurance and building a base level of strength in the rotator cuff and upper back should be the goals of any shoulder-strengthening program. The following four exercises can be used to strengthen the back, or posterior part, of the rotator cuff. Perform each of these exercises slowly and with proper form.

Amazingly, most young players need to use only a 1-pound (0.45-kilogram) weight to start strengthening these muscles. Remember, these are small muscles and tennis players do not need to lift a lot of weight to strengthen them appropriately. In fact, if using too much weight, players will substitute and use muscles other than the rotator cuff to perform the exercise.

Older, more experienced players will experience significant muscular fatigue doing these exercises using a 1.5- or 2-pound (0.7- or 0.9-kilogram) weight if the exercises are done correctly. Control the weight as you lift it (muscles are shortening) and when you lower it (muscles are lengthening) because this prepares the muscle for the specific performance demands encountered during tennis play.

Begin by performing these exercises using three sets of 15 to 20 repetitions. However, you must maintain proper technique when performing these exercises, even on the 20th repetition in the third set. Do not hesitate to do fewer repetitions or sets if you cannot maintain proper technique; it is better to do fewer repetitions correctly than more repetitions incorrectly. As you get stronger, increase the weight in half-pound (0.2-kilogram) increments, but only after you can do all three sets without significant fatigue and without using other parts of your body to compensate. When done correctly, these exercises should not produce pain, just a feeling of burning around the shoulder.

SHOULDER STRENGTHENING EXERCISES

Sidelying External Rotation

Focus: Improve the strength of the external rotator muscles of the shoulder.

Procedure

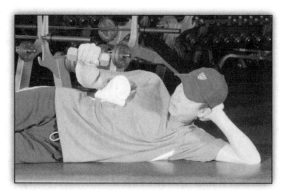

1. Lie on one side with your working arm at your side and a small pillow between your arm and body.
2. Keeping the elbow of your working arm bent and fixed to your side, raise your arm into external rotation until it is just short of pointing straight up (figure 11.5).
3. Slowly lower the arm to the starting position.

Figure 11.5

Shoulder Extension

Focus: Improve the strength of the rotator cuff and scapular muscles.

Procedure

1. Lie facedown on a table with your working arm hanging straight to the floor (figure 11.6a).
2. With your thumb pointed out, raise your arm straight back into extension toward your hip (figure 11.6b).
3. Slowly lower your arm.

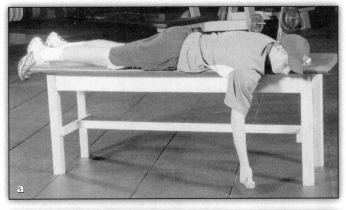

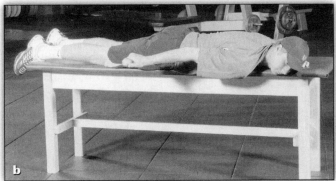

Figure 11.6

Prone Horizontal Abduction

Focus: Improve the strength of the rotator cuff and scapular muscles.

Procedure

1. Lie facedown on a table with your working arm hanging straight to the floor.
2. With your thumb pointed out, raise your arm straight out to the side, parallel to the floor (figure 11.7).
3. Slowly lower your arm.

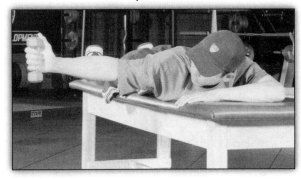

Figure 11.7

Prone 90/90 External Rotation

Focus: Improve the strength of the rotator cuff and scapular muscles.

Procedure

1. Lie facedown on a table with your shoulder abducted to 90 degrees and your arm supported on the table, elbow bent 90 degrees (figure 11.8a). Your hand is hanging off the edge of the table toward the floor.

2. Keeping the shoulder and elbow fixed, externally rotate the shoulder to lift the forearm so that it is parallel to the floor (figure 11.8b).

3. Slowly lower the arm to the starting position.

Other exercises that require elastic tubing or bands can further assist in providing muscle balance to a tennis player's shoulder. The Standing External Rotation exercise works the back, or posterior portion, of the rotator cuff as does the External Rotation at 90 Degrees of Abduction exercise.

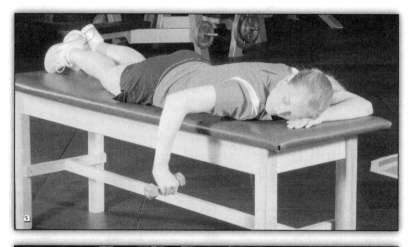

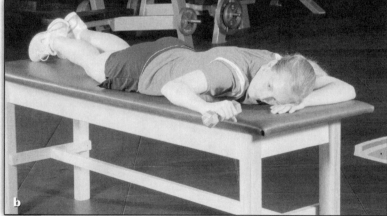

Figure 11.8

Standing External Rotation

DVD

Focus: Improve the strength of the external rotators and scapular stabilizers.

Procedure

1. Stand sideways to a door or secure object. Secure one end of the tubing or band to the doorknob or object at approximately waist height. Your exercising shoulder should be farthest away from the attachment point. Place a rolled towel under the exercising shoulder. Hold the exercising shoulder slightly in front of the body.

2. Begin with slight tension in the band with the hand against the abdomen. Slowly rotate the arm out approximately 90 degrees until your arm points directly in front of you (neutral position) (figure 11.9).

3. Slowly return to the starting position. It is important to work slowly against the resistance of the band in both directions.

Figure 11.9

Standing External Rotation at 90 Degrees of Abduction

Focus: Improve the strength of the external rotators and scapular stabilizers in an elevated position to simulate the service motion.

Procedure

1. Secure one end of a piece of tubing or elastic band just above waist height to a doorknob or stable object. Stand facing the door or attachment point with your exercising shoulder elevated 90 degrees (shoulder level) with your elbow bent 90 degrees (figure 11.10a).

2. From this position with your arm out to the side, move your upper arm and elbow forward about 30 degrees (figure 11.10b). This places the shoulder and upper arm in the proper position and closely simulates the position your arm is in when the racket contacts the ball and follows through during the serve.

3. Before beginning the exercise, maintain the position of your upper arm and lower your forearm until it is horizontal. It may help to use your other hand to support your elbow in the exercise position to better isolate the rotation during the exercise.

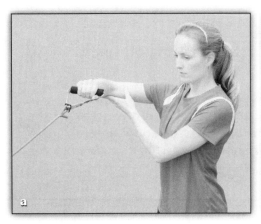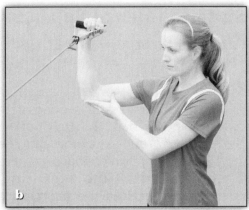

Figure 11.10

4. Slowly move your hand and forearm to a vertical position by externally rotating your shoulder (figure 11.10b). Hold for 1 second in the vertical position and return to the starting position.

Variation: Start from the vertical position as described. Rapidly rotate your shoulder inward to the forearm-horizontal position to stretch the muscles in the back of your shoulder. Immediately after hitting the horizontal position, rapidly return your shoulder to the forearm-vertical position. This is a plyometric-type variation of the traditional external rotation exercise and can be used as a progression or variation.

Note: When performing external rotation with the arm raised to 90 degrees, the upper arm should be approximately 30 degrees forward (as opposed to having the upper arm straight out to the side) for greater comfort and to target the appropriate muscles.

As with the other exercises, perform three sets of 15 to 20 repetitions to build muscular endurance. These exercises are easily performed using elastic tubing; the tubing is inexpensive and can easily be thrown into a tennis bag. Start with a low level of resistance (if using a Thera-Band, this would be the red tubing) and progress to greater resistance when you are able to easily perform three sets of 20 repetitions with proper technique. Avoid using heavy or thick bands or tubing because these create abnormal loads to the shoulder and encourage compensation from other muscles. Recognize that elastic tubing comes in various colors and strengths and a red band made by one company may not offer the same resistance as the red band made by another company. Ask questions when ordering to make sure you get the resistance level that is right for you. Additionally, large quantities of these bands are rather inexpensive, making it possible to buy enough for an entire team to perform these injury prevention exercises.

PLYOMETRIC EXERCISES FOR THE SHOULDER

After progressing through the initial strengthening exercises, move on to exercises that work the muscles more quickly and more closely to the manner in which they will be used during actual tennis play. Plyometrics use a combination of muscle contractions (eccentric contraction followed by a rapid concentric contraction) to develop power and explosiveness. These are advanced exercises and should only be performed once a base level of strength has been established.

Two plyometric exercises for the shoulder are presented in this chapter. In each one, players should use a small 1- or 2-pound (0.45- or 0.9-kilogram) medicine ball to work the back of the rotator cuff while the arm is in the serving position.

PLYOMETRIC SHOULDER EXERCISES

90/90 Prone Plyometric Ball Drop

Focus: Improve the strength of the external rotators and scapular stabilizers in an elevated position to simulate the position of the service motion.

Procedure

1. Lie facedown on a table or exercise ball.

2. Repeatedly drop and quickly catch the plyometric ball (figure 11.11). Be sure to keep the elbow bent 90 degrees and rapidly drop and catch the ball.

3. Do this as fast as possible for 30 seconds, repeating the entire effort two or three times with 15 seconds of rest between sets.

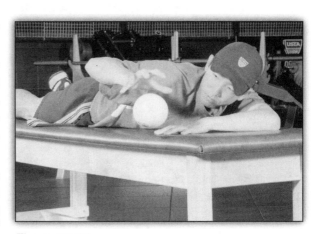

Figure 11.11

90/90 Plyometric Reverse Toss

Focus: Improve the strength of the external rotators and scapular stabilizers in an elevated position to simulate the position of the service motion.

Procedure

1. Kneel with your upper arm out to the side and your elbow bent 90 degrees so that the fingers point to the sky. A partner with a light medicine ball stands 3 to 6 feet (0.9 to 1.8 meters) behind you. The partner should stand closer as you are learning the exercise and move farther away as you gain explosive strength in the rotator cuff and scapular muscles.

2. Your partner throws a light medicine ball slightly in front of your hand (figure 11.12). Catch the ball, decelerate the motion, and immediately throw the ball back forcefully to your partner.

3. Keep your elbow up (approximately 90 degrees) during the exercise.

4. Perform multiple sets of 15 to 20 repetitions.

Variation: Perform this exercise while sitting on an exercise ball.

Figure 11.12

ROLE OF THE SHOULDER BLADE (SCAPULA)

Another area of weakness and vulnerability in a tennis player's shoulder is the shoulder blade, or scapula. Although the ball-and-socket joint is what most people think of when they consider the shoulder, it is important to recognize that the shoulder blade, and how it moves, affects shoulder function as well. To demonstrate this, put your hand on a partner's upper back and ask him or her to raise and lower the arms. You should be able to appreciate how much the shoulder blade moves during normal shoulder motion and why weakness in the muscles that control the shoulder blade can affect shoulder health.

When lifting and lowering the arms, the shoulder blades should remain flush with the torso as they move. Any scapular winging, in which the shoulder blade pops off the torso, signifies weakness in the scapular stabilizers. Prominence of the outline of the shoulder blade, or scapula, on the dominant side indicates the need to strengthen several important muscles that stabilize the scapula: Most important are the serratus anterior and trapezius muscles.

Changes in shoulder posture are also common in tennis players (see figure 11.13). The dominant shoulder is usually lower than the nondominant shoulder. The reason for this difference is unknown, but this adaptation is not thought to place the shoulder at any greater risk for injury.

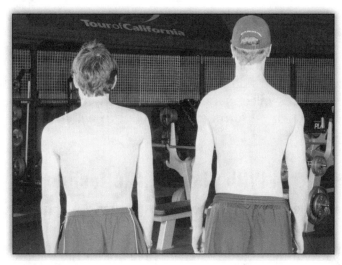

Figure 11.13 Example of shoulder posture differences in left-handed and right-handed tennis players. The player on the left is left handed; the player on the right is right handed. Note how much lower the dominant arm is.

EXERCISES TO STRENGTHEN THE SCAPULAR STABILIZERS

Recommended exercises for increasing the strength of the scapular stabilizers are presented in this section. These include the Seated Row, External Hand Rotation, Step-Up, and Chest Punch. Perform all of these exercises in three sets of 15 to 20 repetitions, with no more than 30 seconds of rest between sets. Perform them slowly and under control to build strength and endurance.

SCAPULAR STABILIZER STRENGTHENING EXERCISES

 ## Seated Row

Focus: Improve the strength of the scapular stabilizers.

Procedure

1. You can perform this exercise using elastic resistance or on various exercise machines. The DVD shows the exercise being performed with elastic tubing while the player is seated on a exercise ball.
2. Pull your hands toward your chest while squeezing your shoulder blades together.
3. Slowly return to the starting position.

   The keys to success in this exercise are squeezing the shoulder blades together as you pull your hands toward your chest and then slowly returning to the starting position. This engages the scapular stabilizers to a greater extent. A common question is whether the elbows should be down or out to the sides during the exercise. It does not matter. The different techniques will engage slightly different muscles in the back and shoulders, but when performed properly, both will help strengthen the scapular stabilizers.

 ## External Rotation With Shoulder Retraction

Focus: Improve the strength of the rotator cuff and scapular stabilizers.

Procedure

1. From a standing position, grasp a piece of elastic band or tubing in your hands (figure 11.14*a*).
2. Rotate your hands out 2 to 3 inches (5 to 7.6 centimeters) then pinch your shoulder blades together (figure 11.14*b*). Hold this position for 1 to 2 seconds.
3. It helps to activate the appropriate muscles if you stick out your chest while squeezing the shoulder blades together.
4. Return to the starting position.

Figure 11.14

Step-Up

Focus: Improve the strength of the serratus anterior, one of the scapular stabilizers.

Procedure

1. Kneel with both hands on the floor in front of a 6- to 8-inch (15- to 20-centimeter) step.
2. One at a time, move your hands up onto the step, making sure to press your upper body away from the floor at the top of the movement. Round your back like a cat in the up position.
3. One at a time, return the hands to the starting position.

Variations

- As you develop greater strength and core stability, perform the exercise on your toes instead of your knees, like in the Push-Up starting position.
- Loop a piece of elastic tubing around your wrists as you perform the exercise (figure 11.15). The band provides resistance as your arms move side to side like during the Monster Walk exercise for the lower body.

Figure 11.15

Note: Although the Step-Up is recommended for the scapular stabilizers, and it does resemble a Push-Up, Push-Ups are not recommended for tennis players. A Push-Up performed so that the chest touches the floor is not appropriate because it places a good deal of stress on the front of the shoulder. In addition, exercises that stress the shoulders by positioning the hands behind the body and exercises that load the shoulders in an overhead position (like a behind-the-neck Lat Pull-Down or a Military Press) are not recommended. The exercises in this book specifically address the imbalances and needs of tennis players and overhead athletes.

 Chest Punch

Focus: Improve the strength of the serratus anterior, one of the scapular stabilizers.

Procedure

1. Lie on your back with your shoulder flexed to 90 degrees and elbow straight. Hold a small medicine ball.
2. Keeping your elbow straight, raise your hands toward the ceiling as far as you can (figure 11.16).
3. Slowly return to the starting position. If you do this correctly, your hand will move only about 6 inches up and down.

Variation: Perform this exercise with one arm at a time. Instead of a medicine ball, you can use other weights, such as a bag of flour or a rock.

Figure 11.16

SUMMARY

Perform the exercises in this chapter to improve shoulder strength, endurance, and flexibility and to protect the shoulder from the repetitive stresses that ultimately lead to muscle imbalances and range-of-motion loss. All of these exercises can be performed several times per week within a periodized training program. Because these exercises can be completed using elastic tubing and light weights, they are ideal for players who are traveling and competing. However, do not perform these exercises before playing tennis. Because you do not want to try to perform tennis stroke patterns with a fatigued rotator cuff, these exercises are best performed after tennis play or on days when you play little tennis. Research has shown that these exercises and stretches are effective in developing shoulder strength and are necessary since simply playing tennis every day does not ensure balanced development of shoulder strength and optimal shoulder range of motion. The incorporation of these exercises into a complete conditioning program will prevent shoulder injury and enhance performance.

Chapter 12

Injury Prevention and Rehabilitation

When asked about a tennis injury, many players will remember the sudden onset of pain during tennis play after one shot or a forceful movement on court. Even though they can remember that one shot or movement, the injury likely resulted not from that one event but rather from the repetitive events that led up to that moment on court when the injury occurred.

Tennis injuries typically fall into the category of overuse injuries, which occur because tennis players constantly exert and produce forces in a repetitive pattern, leading to an accumulation of minor traumas that cause tissue breakdown. For example, overuse injuries can result from the effects on the shoulder of serving thousands of times or the effects on the knees from playing hundreds of points with pivots, twists, and aggressive stops and starts.

Injuries in tennis players fall into two additional categories: acute and chronic. An acute injury is a new injury or complaint from the time it occurs and the relatively short period of time following the start of the injury. A common acute injury suffered by many tennis players is an ankle sprain. A chronic injury is an injury that recurs or repeats because of continued tennis play or a lack of proper rehabilitation. An example of a chronic tennis injury is tennis elbow that has been present for 1 to 2 years and flares up every time the player enters a long, grueling tournament or attends a tennis camp. Acute tennis injuries are much easier to take care of. If treated correctly and quickly, players can prevent an acute injury from becoming chronic.

One of the unique things about the game of tennis is that it stresses nearly all areas of the body. Although most people immediately think of tennis elbow as the ultimate tennis injury, the elbow is only one area commonly injured in tennis players. Injuries can occur to all parts of the body because of the nature and stresses of tennis; however, areas most frequently injured in elite players include the shoulder, lower back, hip, and knee. Data from the U.S. Open Tennis Championships consistently identify the shoulder and back as the leading areas of injury. To address these areas of injury, we have dedicated chapter 7 to improving core stability and chapter 11 to improving shoulder strength, and have included the latest concepts in injury prevention and performance enhancement for those areas. In addition to these chapters, we have provided general injury care and rehabilitation guidelines and specific training recommendations for other areas of the body in order to keep you healthy and injury free.

PREVENTING INJURIES

How do you prevent a tennis injury from occurring? The answer is complex. The best way to prevent an injury is to condition yourself optimally for tennis and prepare your body for the stresses incurred in the game. Many health professionals and tennis coaches used to say, "Play tennis to get in shape." Although tennis certainly provides inherent fitness benefits to the heart, lungs, muscles, and bones, that philosophy doesn't reflect current thinking. The key to preventing injuries and optimizing performance in tennis is clearly "Get in shape to play tennis."

In addition to performing strength and flexibility exercises, using proper technique and selecting equipment appropriate for your playing style and body type also play a critical role. Although many elements of tennis equipment deserve mention, the racket's stiffness, weight, grip size, and string tension are important for injury prevention. Racket stiffness refers to the amount of racket deflection during ball impact. Frame material affects deflection, and therefore racket stiffness. In general, moderately stiff rackets are recommended. Rackets that are either too stiff or too flexible may negatively affect your arm. For example, players with insufficiently developed muscles using a very stiff racket and improper technique may endure excessive shock during impact, which over time may increase their risk of injury. Each major racket manufacturer produces a range of rackets with a variety of stiffness ratings. Pick one near the middle unless otherwise directed by your tennis teaching professional.

In addition to stiffness, the weight of your tennis racket is important. Although a superlight racket is easy to maneuver, playing with one may create greater impact stress because less racket weight is present to absorb the stress of impact, therefore more heavily loading the player's arm. On the other hand, a heavy frame may prove difficult to maneuver and lead to technical challenges and the inability to consistently achieve optimal positions at ball contact. This results in greater muscle use and fatigue. Use a racket that has enough weight to absorb the stress of impact but not enough to make it difficult to maneuver.

The racket's grip size has significant ramifications for injury prevention as well. A grip that is too small forces the forearm muscles to work harder to simply hold the racket. Estimate grip size by gripping the racket and ensuring that enough space exists between the longest finger and the fleshy muscle at the base of the thumb for the little finger of the opposite hand. If the longest finger touches the fleshy muscle, the grip is much too small. Likewise, if there is more than enough space for the little finger, the grip may be too large.

String tension also plays an important part in injury prevention and in optimizing the performance of the racket. Each racket comes with a recommended range of string tensions that the manufacturer feels will cover most of the players who play with that particular frame. Although individual preferences exist, the general rule is that for any given string and racket type, a tighter string tension will produce a more controlled response from the racket, and a looser string tension produces more power from the racket. This is contrary to what many players think. Playing with a racket with a very high string tension may create greater stress on the wrist, elbow, and shoulder and lead to injury.

In addition to string tension, the material and type of string affect performance as well. For injury prevention, strings that are made of many fibers, or filaments, called *coreless multifilament strings,* provide greater resiliency and a generally superior feel. Gut strings are made in this multifilament fashion and are regarded as superior to most other types of nylon strings for playability and resiliency. However, stringing with gut is more costly and often not practical for many young developing players.

Although several aspects of tennis equipment have been quickly summarized here, it is important to discuss all equipment issues with your tennis teaching professional and perhaps a sport scientist. Carefully select all aspects of your racket frame and string type and tension. When recovering from an injury, using gut or coreless multifilament strings, a slightly lower initial string tension (e.g., 3 to 5 pounds [1.4 to 2.3 kilograms]), and frame modification to ensure that proper grip size and weight are present can be important final steps in the recovery process and allow a return to tennis without reinjury or aggravation.

The most important concepts for injury prevention are also important concepts for performance enhancement—flexibility training, strength training, aerobic and anaerobic training, and proper sport biomechanics. Instead of simply summarizing these terms in a general sense, let's apply these concepts to some of the most common tennis injuries.

Shoulder Injuries

Overuse injury of the shoulder is common in tennis players, from elite junior players to senior recreational players. Detailed information regarding the structure and function of the shoulder and exercises for injury prevention and performance enhancement are provided in chapter 11. In addition to the information in that chapter, we discuss here some of the common errors players make.

Typically, tennis players, and other overhead athletes for that matter, use too much weight when performing exercises for the shoulder. Remember, the rotator cuff and scapular muscles are small and can most effectively be worked using light weights or small-diameter elastic tubing in a repetitive fashion, similar to what players encounter in a tennis match.

Another common mistake is lifting weights higher than shoulder level or bringing weights behind the plane of the body. For example, during the final descent phase of the Bench Press, don't lower the weight too far as the bar approaches the chest. This stresses the front of the shoulder as does the end of the descent phase of the standard Fly exercise to work the chest or pectorals. Typically, both the Bench Press and standard Fly exercise are performed while the athlete is lying on his or her back. Although these exercises are not part of a injury prevention program for tennis players, they are general weight training exercises used for the chest and arms by many other types of athletes. In general, we do not recommend these exercises for tennis players. However, if they are included in a tennis-specific training program, the athlete should use a narrow grip and lower the bar only one-half to two-thirds of the way to the chest for the Bench Press, and use a limited motion during the Fly exercise.

Limiting the range of motion by as much as half the typical range specified in weightlifting manuals and texts is often the best advice for tennis players and athletes in overhead sports. Biomechanical analysis of tennis strokes shows that the shoulder is seldom lifted overhead, even during the serve (see figure 12.1). It is safer and less risky to train the rotator cuff muscles using the patterns described in this book.

Figure 12.1 Position of the shoulder during the service motion. Note that the angle of the upper arm to the trunk does not exceed 100 degrees.

Using proper biomechanical stroke technique is another key ingredient that should not be overlooked. Consult your local tennis professional or coach to determine whether your strokes contain movement flaws that may increase your potential for injury and limit your performance.

STROKE TECHNIQUE AND INJURY PREVENTION: OPEN STANCE FOREHAND

In the modern game, the open stance forehand has grown in popularity. Use of the open stance forehand, however, can lead to positions in which the player's upper and lower body are virtually parallel to the baseline at ball contact. Early or premature opening (rotation) of the upper body and trunk can create a lag in which the racket arm trails behind the plane of the body. When this happens during the forehand, it can place excessive stress on the shoulder, particularly the rotator cuff and stabilizing structures, as well as the inside of the elbow. Initially this can lead to tendinitis in the shoulder, but it also places the shoulder at further risk for becoming unstable, making it more susceptible to serious injury.

Adapted with permission from *High-Performance Coaching: The USTA Newsletter for Tennis Coaches,* 2006, Vol. 8., No. 2. page 5.

Trunk and Lower-Back Injuries

Injuries to the trunk and lower back also afflict many tennis players. In a survey of 148 male professional tennis players, 38 percent reported missing a tournament because of a lower-back injury.

The ability to develop power in tennis is often a function of how well the upper and lower parts of the body are connected. The trunk forms a solid unit capable of producing large amounts of power through segmental rotation. The trunk also transfers the power generated by the lower extremities to the arms. This transfer of forces—starting from the feet pushing against the ground; transferring up the legs through the knees and hips and through the trunk; and funneled through the shoulder to the elbow, wrist, and ultimately the racket head—is termed the kinetic-link concept. Training the muscles of the trunk optimizes your ability to apply the kinetic-link system in the generation of power for your strokes. It also is a major factor in preventing injury. Not only does a strong trunk prevent injuries in the lower back, but it also can prevent shoulder and elbow injures by providing a stable platform and force generator, taking stress off the arm.

Changes in the game outlined in chapter 2 have resulted in a greater demand on trunk rotation, particularly in the open stance forehand (see figure 12.2). A powerful open stance forehand requires a huge transfer of force through the trunk with additional power produced by segmental rotation and derotation of the trunk. The amount of trunk rotation used in an open stance forehand and in the inside-out forehand used when stepping or running around a potential backhand is far greater than in the classic-style forehand.

Figure 12.2 Open stance forehand showing how trunk and shoulder rotation generate power and use the entire kinetic chain. Note the amount of trunk rotation.

For proper rotation to safely occur, the abdominals and lower-back muscles must support the vertebrae, discs, and ligaments in the lower back. Specific information on core training is provided in detail in chapter 7.

Flexibility of the trunk and hips is also an important factor in preventing injury to the lower back. Of all the inflexibilities that can develop from playing tennis, tightness in the hamstrings and deep rotators of the hip are particularly harmful for the lower back. Hamstring tightness decreases the motion available at the hips and places more stress on the back by forcing it to move more than if the hamstrings were flexible and hips more mobile. Similarly, a reduction in the range of hip rotation creates greater stress in the lower back and also may increase the risk of injury to the hip joints themselves.

STROKE TECHNIQUE AND INJURY PREVENTION: SERVE

Several of the specific technical aspects of the serve that can lead to injury involve an early opening of the torso and shoulders and inadequate leg drive. As a result of the early opening of the body, players must pull their bodies through the service motion using the abdominal muscles. Additionally, having to pull the arm through the hitting zone can place added stress on the abdominal muscles and shoulder as these areas are forced to make up for the break in the kinetic chain that results from a lack of leg drive and improperly timed rotation of the shoulders and torso. The arm lag position created by the premature opening of the body can place additional loading on the front of the dominant shoulder as well as on the inside of the elbow. Rotator cuff tendinitis and labral tears in the shoulder can result from this excessive loading in the shoulder when in arm lag position during the service motion. Research has shown that a stronger leg drive can reduce the load on the shoulder and elbow.

Adapted by permission from *High-Performance Coaching: The USTA Newsletter for Tennis Coaches,* 2006, Vol. 8., No. 2. page 7.

LOWER-BACK STRETCHES

The stretches listed will ensure that the hamstrings, iliotibial band, hip flexors, and hip rotators are as flexible as they should be. Using the static stretches included in this chapter as an adjunct to the detailed stretches presented in chapter 4 is especially important for players with a history of lower-back and hip injury.

Knees-to-Chest Stretch (page 68)

Hamstring Stretch (page 63)

Hamstring Superstretch (page 64)

Piriformis Stretch (page 66)

Hip Rotator Stretch (page 66)

Spinal Twist (page 68)

Hip Twist (page 65)

Hip Flexor Stretch

Focus: Improve the flexibility of the quadriceps and hip flexor muscles.

Procedure

1. Lie on your back so that the edge of a table or supportive surface hits your legs in the middle of the hamstrings. Bring both knees to your chest.

2. While holding one knee tightly toward your chest, slowly lower the other leg toward the table (figure 12.3). Let the leg hang and flex the knee to 90 degrees. You should feel the stretch in the front of the thigh and hip region.

Note: It may help to have a partner gently press the leg farther down toward the table and floor or bend the knee slightly beyond 90 degrees.

Figure 12.3

Tennis Elbow

One of the injuries most commonly associated with tennis is tennis elbow. Tennis elbow, or humeral epicondylitis, refers to the overuse injury that results from repetitive trauma to the tendons that control movement of the wrist and forearm. The tendons on the outside of the elbow raise the back of the hand toward you (extension) and are the tendons most commonly involved in tennis elbow. This is termed lateral (outside) tennis elbow, and most commonly results from improper technique during backhands, but it can be caused by any tennis stroke because these muscles and tendons undergo stress during all tennis movements using the arm.

Medial, or inside, tennis elbow involves the tendons that bend the wrist down (flexion) or rotate the forearm into a palm-down position (pronation), such as in the serve. This form of tennis tendinitis is more common among highly skilled tennis players, baseball pitchers, and golfers. These muscles and tendons are stressed the most during the forehand and serve. Using technique that does not use the legs, trunk, and arm to produce power but instead uses the elbow, wrist, and hand to produce power, places the player at risk of developing this injury.

The good news about tennis elbow is that in 90 percent of cases, surgery is not required to alleviate it, and it is preventable. The single biggest factor in preventing tennis elbow is using proper biomechanics during the tennis stroke. Strokes that use the muscles in the forearm and wrist to generate power are particularly stressful to the tendons in the elbow. A leading-elbow backhand is a classic example of an improper stroke technique that can cause lateral tennis elbow. Strokes using a "wristy" technique are also particularly bad. To prevent this type of injury, ask your tennis professional to evaluate your strokes.

Two additional strategies for preventing tennis elbow are strengthening and flexibility exercises. Strengthening exercises involve using a light weight—starting with very little weight, 1 to 2 pounds (0.45 to 0.9 kilogram) for young junior players and 3 to 5 pounds (1.4 to 2.3 kilograms) for adults and older juniors—and 30 to 45 repetitions of movement patterns that emphasize the wrist and forearm. The forearm and wrist program described in chapter 8 contains the recommended exercises. These exercises not only improve strength, but they also increase muscular endurance.

Wrist Flexion and Extension (page 137)

Radial and Ulnar Deviation (page 138)

Pronation and Supination (page 139)

Ball Dribble (page 140)

Isolate the movements at the wrist and hand, and avoid using the rest of the upper body or trunk to cheat. Elastic tubing can be used effectively to strengthen these muscles. Adding these exercises to your strengthening program is an important part of preventing tennis elbow and optimizing your performance.

Flexibility is also an important part of preventing tennis elbow. Researchers measured elbow and wrist motion in elite-level junior and senior tennis players and compared the results of the dominant (racket) side to the nondominant side. Because of the effects of repetitive tennis play, the elbow on the dominant side lost the ability to straighten by approximately 5 degrees. Players with elbow injuries often lack as much as 15 degrees of range. This finding is also reported in baseball pitchers.

Two stretches directly address the elbow, forearm, and wrist: the Forearm Flexor Stretch (page 62) and the Forearm Extensor Stretch (page 63). Tennis players should use these stretches to counteract the loss of flexibility (inability to completely straighten the elbow) in the dominant arm that research has shown to exist in both junior and senior tennis players. Perform these stretches both beforeand after tennis play. Remember to hold each stretch for 15 to 20 seconds.

Wrist Injuries

It's not often that doing one thing gives you the added bonus of accomplishing another, but in the case of the exercise program for tennis elbow, this appears to be true. The same strengthening and flexibility exercises players use to prevent tennis elbow also prevent injuries to the wrist. Changes in the game, including stiffer rackets, more extreme forehand grips, more powerful strokes, and the prevalence of fast, hard courts, can increase stress to the wrist. Several top players in the last several years have had serious wrist injuries, which resulted in time away from the game.

STROKE TECHNIQUE AND INJURY PREVENTION: TWO-HANDED BACKHAND

During the preparation phase of the two-handed backhand groundstroke, players often use extreme amounts of downward bending (ulnar deviation) of their dominant side wrists as the racket is prepared to accelerate toward ball

contact. This position is often incorporated as part of the two-handed backhand as players attempt to drop the racket head further below the path of the incoming ball to produce greater topspin. Wrist injuries can occur on either the thumb (radial) side or the little finger (ulnar) side of the wrist. Repetitive use and the forces experienced at the extreme ends of the wrist's range of motion place greater stress on the tendons that cross this joint. A piece of cartilage on the ulnar side of the wrist (the triangular fibrocartilage complex, or TFCC) is loaded when the wrist is put into a position of extreme extension and ulnar deviation. When repeatedly put in this position, the TFCC can actually tear. When this happens, players may experience a clicking feeling in the wrist and pain. This type of injury often requires surgery to correct. Proper biomechanics are an important part of injury prevention.

Adapted by permission from *High-Performance Coaching: The USTA Newsletter for Tennis Coaches*, 2006, Vol. 8., No. 2. page 9.

Increasing strength and endurance of the muscles that cross the wrist helps to protect the wrist as well as the ligaments that help keep the wrist together. Additional exercises for tennis players that can improve the strength and endurance of the muscles that cross the wrist and elbow include Ball Dribble and Wrist Snaps With a Medicine Ball. The Ball Dribble can be performed in 30-second sets to improve endurance, with emphasis on dribbling the ball as quickly as possible. Performing 2 or 3 sets of these exercises will help improve local muscle endurance.

WRIST STRENGTHENING EXERCISES

Ball Dribble

Focus: Improve the strength of the muscles of the forearm and wrist.

Procedure

1. Stand 1 foot (0.3 meter) or so away from a wall or supportive surface.
2. Using a basketball or exercise ball, rapidly bounce the ball back and forth in very small movements against the wall (figure 12.4). The bounce of the ball will only be an inch or two (2.5 to 5 centimeters).

Variation: Vary the dribbling pattern so that the ball moves back and forth in front of you like a windshield wiper.

Figure 12.4

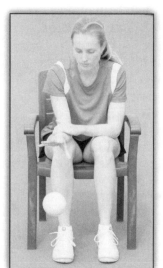

Wrist Snaps With a Medicine Ball

Focus: Improve the explosive strength of the wrist and forearm musculature.

Procedure

1. In a seated position with your forearm resting on your thigh, hold a medicine ball in your hand with your palm facing the floor. Extend your wrist (bend it upward) to prepare to forcefully propel the medicine ball toward the floor (figure 12.5).

Figure 12.5

2. Be sure to keep your forearm against your thigh throughout the exercise because using the elbow and rest of the arm during this exercise reduces the focus on the wrist and forearm muscles.

3. After forcefully throwing the ball by snapping the wrist downward, catch the ball as it pops back up into your hand and repeat.

Knee Injuries

One final area to discuss is injury to the knee joint. Tennis places a great deal of stress on the knee joints because of the bending, quick starts and stops, and explosive accelerations required for top level play. Because tennis is technically a noncontact sport, the bone-crushing knee injuries we've come to equate with football or skiing are not all that prevalent. Instead, injures to the knee (patellofemoral joint) are probably the most disabling among tennis players. The knee cap, or patella, rides in a shallow groove at the end of the thigh bone, or femur. If a player endures repeated stress to the legs during tennis play in the absence of sufficient strength and endurance of the thigh muscles (especially the quadriceps), the knee cap can become irritated. This irritation is caused by the lack of support from the surrounding muscles as they fatigue because a knee cap without muscular support will not glide properly in the groove in the end of the thigh bone. This repeated irritation can wear down the back of the knee cap and produce significant pain. Braces can support the knee cap, but the best support comes from the muscles.

Preventing knee injuries focuses on two main strategies: improving flexibility and improving strength. To strengthen your knees, use the exercises described in chapter 8. When performing exercises for the knees, limit the movement pattern to decrease the stress to the knees. Pressure between the knee cap and the end of the femur, or thigh bone, is greatest when the knee is bent between 45 and 60 degrees during leg extension–type exercises (see figure 8.3, page 125). Because this part of the movement is particularly stressful, players experiencing knee pain or who have a history of knee injury should avoid it.

Players with achy knees should also avoid deep squat, lunge, and leg press movements in which the knees bend more than 90 degrees. These exercises cause a large amount of stress while the muscles are being strengthened and should be avoided. The following are the key exercises and stretches to help prevent injury to the knees.

KNEE STRENGTHENING EXERCISES

Leg Press (page 122)

Partial Squat (page 124)

Lunge (multidirectional variation) (page 127)

Injury Prevention and Rehabilitation ◆ 197

Multihip (page 128)

Leg Extension (partial range if indicated) (page 124)

Hamstring Curl (page 130)

Leg Raise With Cuff Weight

Focus: Improve the strength of the quadriceps and hip flexors; rehabilitate the knee after surgery or injury.

Procedure

1. Because no actual motion at the knee occurs during this exercise, it is usually well tolerated. Lie on your back with one leg straight out in front of you. Place a cuff weight onto the ankle of that leg. Keeping the foot on the floor, bend the other knee to approximately 90 degrees to decrease the stress on your lower back.

2. Tighten your thigh muscle and raise your leg about 6 inches (15 centimeters) off the ground, keeping your knee straight. Hold for 1 count before slowly returning to the start position.

3. Repeat for multiple sets of 10 to 15 repetitions.

KNEE STRETCHES

Hamstring Stretch (page 63)

Hamstring Superstretch (page 64)

Quadriceps Stretch (page 64)

Hip Rotator Stretch (page 66)

Iliotibial Band Stretch (page 67)

Common strengthening exercises, such as the Lunge and Squat, deserve further discussion because these exercises involve a key component for all tennis players—balance. Both the Lunge and Squat can be made more difficult by using foam pads, which provide a less stable exercise surface. This forces the player to concentrate and challenge more muscle groups in the lower body and trunk while performing the exercise and assists in the development of balance, an important part of any tennis player's game. When performing the Lunge and Squat exercises, do not bend the knees too far, which puts excessive loads on the knee cap, and maintain proper knee alignment during the exercise movement. The knee should be aligned over the foot during the exercise. Figure 12.6*a* shows a player doing a Squat on a balance platform, maintaining proper knee alignment during the descent phase. Figure 12.6*b* shows improper alignment, characterized by an inward movement of the knee, increasing the angle and stress at the knee. Performing exercises with this improper movement is not only potentially harmful, but it may also lead to promoting this movement during on-court movements while playing tennis. Athletes should pay special attention to using proper technique during these exercises. This is imperative for injury prevention and optimizing performance and should be part of every tennis player's exercise program.

Figure 12.6   One-leg squat on unstable surface or balance pad: *(a)* correct knee alignment; *(b)* incorrect knee alignment; note inward angulation of the standing knee.

TREATING INJURIES

How do you manage a tennis injury once it has occurred? Use the mnemonic PRICE to help you remember the steps for safely treating an acute tennis injury.

P—protect

R—rest

I—ice

C—compress

E—elevate

Protect the injured area from further stress. That doesn't mean that every injury must be placed in a cast or kept from moving at all. Instead, minimize or eliminate the stresses that caused the injury.

Rest the area to allow healing and prevent further injury.

Apply *ice* to the injured area to minimize swelling and decrease pain and inflammation. Typically, you can apply ice can to an injured area for

10 to 20 minutes. This constricts the blood vessels in the area. Ice can be applied frequently immediately after an injury. However, alternate periods without ice application to prevent blanching, or stressing the skin. For example, many players ice their ankles for 20 minutes every few hours immediately after an ankle sprain. Application of ice continues for several days. A decrease in pain and swelling, rather than following a rigid time frame, indicate when to discontinue icing. In general, use ice after an acute injury until someone such as a physician, therapist, or trainer with knowledge of treatment and rehabilitation further directs you. Using heat after an injury is not typically recommended and may increase swelling by dilating the blood vessels.

Compression works along with the ice to prevent swelling. It typically is applied as an elastic bandage wrapped around the injured area. The compression wrap also provides support to the injured area.

Elevation applies mainly to injuries to the knee, ankle, foot, elbow, wrist, and hand. Place the injured area higher than the heart. This helps prevent swelling, or pooling of fluids, in the injured area and uses gravity to decrease the swelling that has already occurred.

After applying the principles of PRICE to initially treat a tennis injury, follow up with an evaluation of your injury by a medical professional. This is recommended for any tennis injury, whether it's a first-time ankle sprain or a chronic problem with your shoulder.

PREVENTING HEAT-RELATED ILLNESS

One final area to discuss is preventing heat illness. Although not a musculoskeletal injury, heat stress is a common ailment during tennis play. It can include heat cramps, heat exhaustion, and, most seriously, heatstroke. The most widely recommended prevention strategies for heat illness are proper hydration and nutritional intake.

While playing tennis in the heat, the body's primary cooling mechanism is sweating. Sweat rates in male and female tennis players can range from 0.5 and 2.5 liters per hour depending on fitness level, environmental temperature, and hydration status.

In addition to water, electrolytes are lost in sweat. Sodium and chloride are the primary electrolytes lost during sweating, but potassium and magnesium are also lost. Contrary to popular belief, sport scientists now believe that sodium loss through heavy sweating may be the largest contributor to heat cramps.

Thirst is clearly not an adequate stimulus for hydration; a person can lose 1.5 liters of water before feeling thirsty. Therefore, proper hydration involves drinking before you are thirsty and properly hydrating before tennis play. Drinking fluids the night before and early in the day before tennis play improves a player's prematch hydration status.

During actual tennis play, drink during every changeover, even if you are not thirsty. Remember, the thirst mechanism is not a reliable indicator of fluid need. Hydrate using water or a suitable fluid replacement beverage that replaces the electrolytes lost during periods of heavy sweating. Always use a fluid replacement beverage that you have tried in practice. Never try a replacement beverage for the first time during a match.

During periods of heavy sweat loss, replacement of sodium becomes important. Salt pills are not recommended and irritate the stomach and intestine. Therefore, salt foods more heavily, and use a previously tested electrolyte replacement beverage to replace electrolytes along with water. Whenever possible, let yourself adjust to the climate you will play in before the actual competition. It takes 7 to 10 days to fully acclimate to a new climate. Benefits of acclimation include better sweat rates, sweating earlier in response to heat stress, and less sodium loss at the sweat gland.

USTA FLUID RECOMMENDATIONS

Drink cool water or sport drinks during play. Sport drinks are especially helpful during long matches, in hot weather, and for recovery after play. Use a similar hydration routine before, during, and after practice.

Before Play
- Drink 12 to 16 ounces (350 to 470 milliliters) about 1 hour before play begins.
- Drink fluids often throughout the day.
- Prepare at least 2 quarts (64 ounces [approximately 2 liters]) to drink during play. Sport drinks are preferable for long matches or during play in hot weather.

During Play
- Drink 4 to 8 ounces (120 to 240 milliliters) (4 to 8 normal swallows) after the warm-up and during every changeover.
- Many players like to drink a 2:1 mixture of sport drink and water.
- For some players, fluid requirements may be higher in very hot or humid environments.

After Play
- Weigh yourself before and after play and drink 20 to 24 ounces (590 to 680 milliliters) of fluid for every pound (0.45 kilogram) of postplay body weight lost.
- Immediately begin to replace fluid, electrolytes, and carbohydrate with water, other fluids (e.g., juice, sport drinks), and food. Sport drinks are effective if you are going to play again soon.
- Consider adding salt to your food or drinks if sweat losses were extensive.

USTA Sport Science Committee, Summer 2003.

SUMMARY

Following a total conditioning program for tennis will help prevent injury and optimize performance. Your knowledge of the information presented in this chapter will provide you with the strategies to prevent heat illness through proper hydration, as well as minimize the chances of common musculoskeletal injuries.

Index

The italicized *f* and *t* following page numbers refers to figures and tables that illustrate the topic.

A

abdominal muscles, 101
acceleration and deceleration, 90*f*–91*f*
aerobic endurance
    about, 6, 40, 145–149
    1.5-Mile Run test, 40*t*–41
    training, 150–152
aggressive baseline game style, 10
agility
    about, 4, 35, 71
    positioning, 72–73
    surfaces, 71–72
agility and speed tests
    20-Yard Dash, 36–37*t*
    Hexagon Test, 35–36*ft*
    Sideways Shuffle, 38*t*
    Spider Run Test, 7*f*, 37*f*–38*t*
agility drills
    Condensed Deuce Court, 84–85
    Court Widths or 17s, 81
    Cross Cones, 78*f*
    Diagonal Repeater, 83*f*
    Figure-8, 79*f*
    Forehand and Backhand Agility, 84
    Forward and Backward, 81
    Forward and Backward Alley Drill, 76*f*
    Forward and Backward Cone Slalom, 77
    Four-Cone Square, 79*f*–80
    Horizontal Repeater, 82*f*
    Lateral Alley Drill, 75*f*
    Lateral Cone Slalom, 76–77*f*
    Medicine Ball Tennis, 86
    Mini Tennis Z-Ball, 85*f*
    Service-Box Crossover, 80*f*
    Spider Run, 77–78*f*
    Vertical Repeater, 82*f*
    Volley Drill, 83*f*–84
all-court game style, 10
anaerobic fitness, 6, 145–151, 147–149

B

back, lower-, stretches, 191, 192*f*
backhand groundstroke, one-handed, 15*t*, 121*t*
backhand groundstroke, two-handed, 121*t*, 194*f*
back muscles, 97, 98, 189–191*f*, 190*f*
ballistic stretching, 69
Blake, James, 114*f*
body composition
    about, 5, 39
    Skinfold test, 39
body-fat percentage, 5

C

carbohydrates, 5
cardiorespiratory fitness, 162
Clijsters, Kim, 2*f*, 148*f*, 189*f*
conditioning program
    designing, 7–8, 153–154
    periodization training, 154–165
    on the road, 164
    testing and tracking, 6–7
contract-relax stretching, 69
core stability tests
    Core Stability, 25–26*f*
    Sit-Up, 24*f*–25*t*
core stability training
    abdominal, 101–103
    about, 97–101
    advanced, 110–112
    co-contraction exercises, 106–107
    lower back, 108–110
    trunk rotation, 104–106
core stability training drills
    Abdominal Curl on Exercise Ball, 100–101*f*
    Arm and Leg Extension, 109*f*
    Cobra, 109–110*f*
    Dead Bug, 103*f*
    Diagonal Leg Tuck, 112f

core stability training drills *(continued)*
    Drawing In, 101*f*
    Knees to Chest, 111
    Knees to Chest With Rotation, 111*f*
    Lunge With Rotation, 106
    Russian Twist, 105*f*
    Seated Ball Rotation, 104*f*
    Side Plange, 107*f*
    Superman, 108*f*
    TV Watching, 106–107*f*
counterpunching game style, 10

D

diet and nutrition, 5
dynamic balance, 5–6
dynamic stretching drills
    about, 49–50
    Arm Hugs, 59*f*
    Backward Lunge With Trunk
        Rotation, 58*f*
    Backward Step Over, 59*f*
    Butt Kick, 58*f*
    Carioca, 52*f*
    Figure-4 Tuck, 54*f*
    Frankenstein Walk, 55*f*
    Front Lunge, 56*f*
    High Step Trunk Rotation, 56*f*
    Inverted Hamstrings, 54*f*
    Jogging With Arm Circles, 51
    Knee-Hug Lunge, 53*f*
    Knee-to-Chest Tuck, 52*f*
    Side Lunge, 55*f*
    Side Step With Arm Crosses, 51
    Torso Rotation, 57*f*
    Torso Rotation With Squat, 57*f*

E

energy systems, 148–149
equipment, 71

F

Federer, Roger, 14*f*
flexibility
    about, 18
    demands, 2–3
    training, 44–47*f*, 46*f*
flexibility tests
    Hamstring Flexibility, 20*ft*
    Hip Flexor Flexibility, 19*f*–20
    Hip Rotation, 21*f*

    Quadriceps Flexibility, 22*f*
    Shoulder Flexibility Test, 22–23*f*
    Sit-and-Reach, 18–19*t*
flexibility training routine
    dynamic stretching, 49–59
    other methods, 69
    static stretching, 60–68
footwork. *see* agility
forehand groundstroke, 15*t*, 120*t*

G

game styles, 10

H

Hingis, Martina, 160*f*
hips, 97
hydration, 199–200

I

injuries
    chronic nature of, 185–186
    heat-related, 199–200
    knee, 196–198
    preventing, 186–187
    shoulder, 167–168, 187–188*f*, 189*f*
    tennis elbow, 192–193
    treatment, 198–199
    trunk and lower-back, 189–191*f*,
        190*f*
    wrist, 194*f*–196

J

Jumping Into Plyometrics (Chu), 88

K

knee strengthening and stretches,
    196–197

M

Mauresmo, Amelie, 154*f*
maximal heart rate, 145–146
muscles, in stroke techniques, 14–16*t*,
    15*t*, 121*t*

N

Nadal, Rafael, 5*f*

O

overhead stroke, 16*t*, 121*t*

P

pelvis, 97

periodization training
    about, 154–155
    on the road, 164
    sample training, 162f–164
    for tennis, 158–161
    training specificity, 161–162
Petrova, Nadia, 191f
plyometrics, 85–86
power, about, 31
power tests
    Medicine Ball Toss, Forehand and
        Backhand, 32–33ft
    Medicine Ball Toss, Overhead and
        Reverse Overhead, 34ft–35t
    Vertical Jump, 31f–32t
power training. see strength and
        power training

Q
Querrey, Sam, 99f
quickness. see speed and quickness

R
reaction time, 87–88
resistance training. see strength and
        power training
rest periods, 159–161
Roddick, Andy, 3f

S
scapular stabilizer strengthening
    Chest Punch, 182f
    External Hand Rotation, 179–181f
    Seated Row, 180
    Step-Up, 181f–182
season length, 159
serve-and-volley game style, 10
service stroke, 16t, 96–97, 121t
Sharapova, Maria, 10f
shoulder
    anatomy and structure, 167–168f
    injuries, 169–170
    scapular stabilizer strengthening,
        180–182
    shoulder blade role, 178–179
    special characteristics for tennis,
        168–169
shoulder exercises, plyometric
    90/90 Prone Plyometric Ball Drop,
        177f

90/90 Prone Plyometric Reverse
        Toss, 178f
shoulder strengthening exercises
    External Rotation at 90 Degrees of
        Abduction, 175–176f
    Prone 90/90 External Rotation, 174
    Prone Horizontal Abduction, 173f
    Shoulder Extension, 172–173
    Sidelying External Rotation, 172f
    Standing External Rotation, 175f
shoulder stretches, preventive
    Cross-Arm Stretch, 170f
    Sleeper Stretch, 171f
speed. see speed and quickness
speed and quickness
    about, 4, 87–88
    acceleration and deceleration,
        90f–91f
    quickness, 88
    reaction time, 88–89
    running mechanics and form,
        91–92
speed and quickness drills
    Butt Kick, 94
    High-Knee March, No Arms, 92f
    High-Knee March, With Arms, 93f
    High-Knee Run, No Arms, 95f
    High-Knee Run, With Arms, 95f
    Skip, 93
    Skip With Leg Extension, 94f
speed tests. see agility and speed tests
split step, 73f
stability, 5–6
static stretching drills
    about, 60–61
    Calf Stretch, 67f
    Forearm Extensor Stretch, 63f
    Forearm Flexor Stretch, 62f
    Hamstring Stretch, 63f
    Hamstring Superstretch, 64f
    hip and leg, 63–67
    Hip Rotator Stretch, 66f
    Hip Twist, 65f
    Iliotibial Band Stretch, 67f
    Knees-to-Chest Stretch, 68f
    Piriformis Stretch, 66f
    Posterior Shoulder Stretch, 61
    Quadriceps Stretch, 63f
    Seated Groin Stretch, 65f

static stretching drills   *(continued)*
   shoulder and arm, 61–63
   Sleeper Stretch, 62*f*
   Spinal Twist, 68*f*
   trunk, 68
strength and muscular endurance
   about, 23
   demands, 3–4, 4
strength and muscular endurance tests
   Core Stability, 25–26*f*
   Grip Strength, 30*ft*
   One-Leg Stability Test, 29*f*–30
   Push-Up, 26–27*ft*
   Scapular Stabilization, 28–29*f*
   Shoulder External Rotation Manual
      Muscle Test, 27–28*f*
   Sit-Up, 24*f*–25*t*
strength and power training
   about, 113
   back, 131–132
   designing training program, 117–
      120
   forearm and wrist, 137–140
   lower-body, 122–130
   morphological adaptations, 116–
      117
   muscles used in strokes, 121*t*
   neural adaptations, 116
   plyometric medicine ball program,
      142–143
   precautions, 122
   shoulder, 140–141
   single-joint *vs.* multiple-joint,
      115–116
   trunk, 131–132
   types of resistance training, 113–115
strength and power training drills
   Back Extension, 131
   Backhand Toss, 142–143
   Ball Dribble, 140*f*
   Bent-Over Row, 134*f*
   Biceps Curl, 136*f*
   Calf Raise, 128*f*
   Core Chest Press, 135*f*
   Elastic Band Kick, 129*f*–130

   Forearm Flexion and Extension,
      137*f*
   Forehand Toss, 142
   Hamstring Curl, 130*f*
   Lat Pull-Down, 133*f*
   Leg Extension, 124
   Leg Press, 122–123*f*
   Low-to-High Chop, 126*f*–127
   Lunge, 127*f*
   Monster Walk, 129*f*
   Multihip, 128
   Partial Squat, 126–127*f*
   Plyometric Chest Pass, 142
   Plyometric Leg Press, 123–124
   Plyometric Stepover, 125–126*f*
   Pronation and Supination, 139*f*
   Prone Fly, 140–141*f*
   Radial and Ulnar Deviation, 138*f*
   Seated Row, 133–134*f*
   Shoulder Punch, 141*f*
   Shrug, 140
   Triceps Extension, 136*f*
   Trunk Rotation, 132
stretching drills. *see* dynamic
      stretching drills; static
      stretching drills

T
tennis
   about, 1–2
   coordinated movement in, 13*f*–14
   game style, 10
   movement demands, 11
   muscle actions, 11–13, 15*t*–16*t*
   physical demands of, 2–7
Tennis Tactics (Human Kinetics), 10
tournament length, 159
trunk muscles, 95–96, 189–191*f*, 190*f*

W
warm-up. *see also* dynamic stretching
      drills; static stretching drills
   about, 43–44, 47–49
Williams, Serena, 4*f*
Williams, Venus, 191*f*
wrist strengthening exercises, 190–192

About the Authors

E. Paul Roetert, Ph.D., is the Managing Director of the United States Tennis Association's Player Development Program. In addition, he serves as Tournament Director of the U.S. Open Junior Tennis Championships. Before re-joining the USTA in November, 2001, Roetert spent two years as the Executive Director of the American Sport Education Program. Prior to that position he spent eleven years as the Administrator of Sport Science for the USTA where he developed the sport science program. He also served as Vice Chairman of the sport science committee.

Roetert has published extensively in the field of tennis, including two books, 16 book chapters and well over 100 articles. He is a Fellow in the American College of Sports Medicine (ACSM), a Master Professional with the United States Professional Tennis Association (USPTA) and an Honorary Member of the Professional Registry (PTR). In 1998 he received the PTR's Plagenhoef Award for sport science; in 1999 the Editorial Excellence Award from the National Strength and Conditioning Association for his work on the Journal of Strength and Conditioning and Research; and in 2000 the Outstanding Alumni award from the University of Connecticut. He is also the 2002 Educational Merit Award recipient from the International Tennis Hall of Fame for outstanding service to the game of tennis.

Roetert holds a Ph.D. in biomechanics from the University of Connecticut. Originally from the Netherlands, he and his wife Barbara reside in Miami, Florida.

Todd S. Ellenbecker, DPT, MS, SCS, OCS, CSCS, is the clinic director at Physiotherapy Associates Scottsdale Sports Clinic in Scottsdale, Arizona. A licensed physical therapist, he has researched and taught in the field for 18 years.

Ellenbecker is certified by the American Physical Therapy Association (APTA) as both a sports clinical specialist and orthopedic clinical specialist. The APTA also awarded him its Sports Physical Therapy Clinical Teaching Award in 1999. He was chairman of the APTA's Shoulder Special Interest Group and is a manuscript reviewer for the *Journal of Orthopaedic and Sports Physical Therapy* and the *American Journal of Sports Medicine.*

In addition, Ellenbecker is a member of the American College of Sports Medicine (ACSM) and the United States Professional Tennis Association (USPTA). He is chairman of the USTA's National Sport Science Committee and is a certified strength and conditioning specialist through the National Strength and Conditioning Association (NSCA). In 2003, the NSCA named him the Sports Medicine Professional of the Year.

He has served as a member of the Thera-Band research advisory committee and is coauthor of *The Scientific and Clinical Application of Elastic Resistance*. He also has cowritten *The Elbow in Sport, World-Class Tennis Technique*, and *Closed Kinetic Chain Exercise*.

Ellenbecker lives in Scottsdale, Arizona, with his wife, Gail.

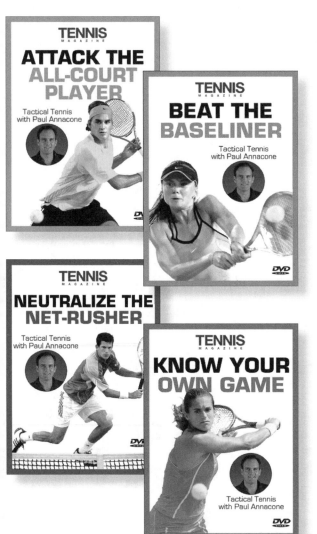